Through Another Lens

Reflections on the Gospels

YEAR A

Barbara Jean Franklin, ASC

Liguori
LIGUORI, MISSOURI

Imprimi Potest: Thomas D. Picton, C.Ss.R.
Provincial, Denver Province, The Redemptorists

Published by Liguori Publications
Liguori, Missouri 63057
To order, call 800-325-9521, or visit www.liguori.org.

Copyright © 2010 Barbara Jean Franklin, ASC

Library of Congress Cataloging-in-Publication Data
Franklin, Barbara, (Barbara Jean)
   Through another lens : reflections on the Gospels, Year A / Barbara Jean Franklin.—1st ed.
   p. cm.
   ISBN 978-0-7648-1908-7
   1. Church year meditations. 2. Bible. N.T. Gospels—Meditations. 3. Catholic Church—Prayers and devotions. 4. Catholic Church. Lectionary for Mass (U.S.). Year A. I. Title.
   BX2170.C55F73 2010
   242'.3—dc22

                              2010020286

Additional copyright acknowledgments are listed on pages v-vi.

Liguori Publications, a nonprofit corporation, is an apostolate of the Redemptorists. To learn more about the Redemptorists, visit Redemptorists.com.

Printed in the United States of America
14 13 12 11 10   5 4 3 2 1
First edition

Contents

Acknowledgments

Excerpt from "Two Pilgrims at Harvest Time" by Clare Boehmer, ASC, from unpublished 1974 text. Used by permission of author.

Excerpts from "—and Me, Raissa", "The Other Grandmother", and "Sara, Peter's Mother-in-Law" by Kathy Coffey in *Hidden Women of the Gospels,* (New York: Crossroads Publishing Co., 1996). Copyright © 1996 by Kathy Coffey. Used by permission of Orbis.

Excerpt from "Covenant" by Margaret Halask in *Life Through a Poet's Eyes,* compiled by David L. Fleming, SJ. Copyright © 1999 Review for Religious. All rights reserved. Used by permission.

Excerpts from "He Asked for Charity" by Francis of Assisi, "The Wind Will Show Its Kindness" by Meister Eckhart, and "Trying to Work In" and "It Acts Like Love" by Rabia, in *Love Poems From God,* trans. Daniel Ladinsky (New York: Penguin Compass, 2002). Copyright © Daniel Ladinsky, 2002. Used by permission.

Excerpt from "A man from Phrygia, on Pentecost" from A CRY LIKE A BELL WHEATON LITERARY SERIES by Madeleine L'Engle, copyright © 2000 by Crosswicks, Ltd. Excerpts from "Advent, 1971" and "Sonnet, Trinity 18" from THE WEATHER OF THE HEART WHEATON LITERARY by Madeleine L'Engle, copyright © 2000 by Crosswicks, Ltd. All used by permission of WaterBrook Multnomah, an imprint of the Crown Publishing Group, a division of Random House, Inc.

Excerpt from "The Servant-Girl at Emmaus (A Painting by Velázquez)" by Denise Levertov from BREATHING THE WATER, copyright ©1987 by Denise Levertov. Excerpt from "Poetics of Faith" by Denise Levertov from SANDS OF THE WELL, copyright ©1996 by Denise Levertov. Excerpt from "The Avowal" by Denise Levertov in THE STREAM AND THE SAPPHIRE, copyright ©1984 by Denise Levertov. All reprinted by permission of New Directions Publishing Corp.

Excerpt from "And the Children of Birmingham" by Thomas Merton, from THE COLLECTED POEMS OF THOMAS MERTON, copyright © 1963 by The Abbey of Gethsemani. Excerpt from "The Flight Into Egypt" by Thomas Merton, from THE COLLECTED POEMS OF THOMAS MERTON, copyright © 1944 by The Abbey of Gethsemani. Excerpt from "The House of Caiphas" by Thomas Merton, from THE COLLECTED POEMS OF THOMAS MERTON, copyright © 1946 by The Abbey of Gethsemani. All reprinted by permission of New Directions Publishing Corp.

Excerpts from "A Prayer for Wholehearted Commitment", "Prayer for a Nun in a Wheelchair", and "Sharon's Christmas Prayer" by John Shea in *The Hour of the Unexpected*, (Niles, IL: Argus Communications, 1977). Copyright © 1977 by John Shea. Used by permission of author.

Excerpt from "The Borderland—9" by Rabindranath Tagore in RABI-NDRANATH TAGORE: SELECTED POEMS, trans. by William Radice (Penguin, 1985), 107. Copyright © William Radice, 1985. Used by permission of Penguin Group.

Excerpt from "The Wounding" by Elizabeth-Anne Vanek in *Woman Dreamer: A Collection of Poems*. Copyright © 1989 by Elizabeth-Anne Vanek. All rights reserved. Used by permission of author.

Excerpts from "A Different Kind of King", "A Woman's Journey in Discipleship", "Beloved Son", "Companion", "Easter Witnesses", "Emmanuel: God With Us", "Expanding the Mission", "I Am With You Always", "Legacy", and "Theophany" from *INCARNATION: New and Selected Poems for Spiritual Reflection*, by Irene Zimmerman. Copyright © 2004 by Irene Zimmerman. All rights reserved. Used by permission of Cowley Publications, an imprint of the Rowman & Littlefield Publishing Group, 4501 Forbes Blvd., Suite 200, Lanham, MD 20706.

Advent

First Sunday of Advent
Matthew 24:37-44

✤ It seems easier to begin Advent focusing on the coming of an innocent child born in a stable in an obscure town called Bethlehem. Even images of a stable floor messy with dirty straw, the smell of draft animals, and a chorus of braying donkeys have a certain charm compared to today's Gospel passage.

Matthew presents us with images of Noah and the flood and of thieves breaking into homes. These images are part of Matthew's long list of signs of the times—signs of God's in-breaking reign—and they are not part of our traditional Christmas tableaus. Matthew's intent is not to comfort but to disturb his readers, to challenge his readers to help bring about God's reign. Our Advent journey is not about the re-creation of Bethlehem scenes but about the re-creation of our Christian lives.

William Butler Yeats has a complex poem called "The Second Coming," that can be helpful in charting our course. This poem has layers of meaning and many nuances that have, at times, been offensive to some orthodox Christians. However, Matthew tells us it is important to read the signs of the times, and Yeats has imagery in his poem that gives us much for reflection as responsible Christians.

Turning and turning in the widening gyre
The falcon cannot hear the falconer;
Things fall apart; the centre cannot hold;
Mere anarchy is loosed upon the world,
The blood-dimmed tide is loosed, and everywhere
The ceremony of innocence is drowned;
The best lack all conviction, while the worst
Are full of passionate intensity.

Surely some revelation is at hand;
Surely the Second Coming is at hand.
The Second Coming! Hardly are those words out
When a vast image of Spiritus Mundi
Troubles my sight: somewhere in sands of the desert
A shape with lion body and the head of a man,
A gaze blank and pitiless as the sun,
Is moving its slow thighs, while all about it
Reel shadows of the indignant desert birds.
The darkness drops again; but now I know
That twenty centuries of stony sleep
Were vexed to nightmare by a rocking cradle,
And what rough beast, its hour come round at last,
Slouches toward Bethlehem to be born?[1]

Like today's Gospel passage, the poem has a sense of immediacy. Yeats wrote his poem in 1919, following World War I, yet we, too, live in times of political upheaval and human and ecological distress. Particularly at chronological mileposts like the beginning of Advent we think of history as an ever-expanding spiral and sometimes wonder if we've progressed on a spiral or only repeated the same circuit.

The poem's opening image of the falcon's widening gyre, its distancing out of earshot of the falconer so that "Things fall apart; the centre cannot hold" raises questions for each of us about whether we have moved from our center and lost our moral compass. With

Yeats we can also question our society: Are the best paralyzed by "lack [of] conviction" and the worst "full of passionate intensity"? Our own responses to these questions determine whether this first stanza is about a foreboding doom or about Matthew's warning, "you also must be ready."

In the second stanza the poet surmises that, because of the conditions he described in the first, "the Second Coming is at hand." With the mention of Bethlehem in the last line, Yeats connects the Second Coming to that of Christ. While in Yeats' universe this is not necessarily the second coming of Christ about which Matthew writes, the poet gives us reason to believe things can be different. Yeats' term, *"Spiritus Mundi,"* literally "the spirit of the world," can be moved in a different direction. The beast is disturbed by "indignant desert birds." These are the people who mirror God's own self-giving, who stand up to the *status quo,* who are not passive to the elements of society who promote war and turn a deaf ear to the needs of humanity and of our planet.

Yeats may have concluded their task was impossible. But that is what we are invited to reflect on as we begin a new Church year. Manger scenes, religious practices, and generous donations can give us a false sense of security.

Matthew, instead, challenges us to prepare for surprises—to take a good hard look at our human and spiritual journey. We must be shaken to the depths so we can wake up to the truth of ourselves. We hope to awaken to find ourselves, not on the same familiar circuit, but on an ever-widening and inclusive spiral that makes it clear to all that Christ has come into our world. "Therefore you also must be ready, for the Son of Man is coming at an unexpected hour."

Second Sunday of Advent
Matthew 3:1–12

✤ Today John the Baptist bursts into our tidy lives proclaiming, "Repent, for the kingdom of heaven has come near....Prepare the way of the Lord, make his paths straight." Maybe these words are not so startling for those who took very seriously Matthew's message about the unexpected coming of the Son of Man which we heard last week.

Perhaps this past week has been an awakening to God's presence in our world and there has been a sincere effort at recognizing and confessing sin. We might even find ourselves lining up with the people of Jerusalem and all of Judea to be baptized by John in the river Jordan. So, what shall we do with the rest of Advent?

John the Baptist would be quick to intervene and ask if the reforming power of God's coming has really penetrated our lives. What evidence do we find in our interior motivations and external actions to prove our reformation? Would John see us approach and say to us what he said to the Pharisees and Sadducees in today's Gospel passage: "You brood of vipers!" I heard the equivalent of those words one day when I read in a parish bulletin an item titled, "Pray for the conversion of our leaders." It was an invitation to be part of an overnight vigil of prayer for the conversion of our nation's leaders so they would reverse the ruling that legalized abortion.

To my surprise, what I felt invited to was to pray first for my own conversion, not specific to any particular law or social injustice, but to the many ways I get caught up in seeing how civil and religious leaders need to change while I overlook the many unjust relationships and self-centered actions that define my life. I find it easy to throw light on the sinfulness of society, but do I really want the Light that John heralded to shine on the crevices of my life?

Of course you are the messenger, you who
Shed the grey brightness which the sun breaks
through.
As when pale dawn provokes the birds to play
Their music glorifies the shape of day,
So your birth violates your father's tongue
Till, from his lips, a shriek of praise is wrung.
And as the sun burns red when the last gleam
Of styptic dawn admits a blood-red stream,
Your blood, too, gushes on the world whose fate
The sun you herald will illuminate.[2]

Like Matthew, the poet's John the Baptist cuts to the very heart of our baptism. Matthew's John says, "now the ax is lying at the root of the trees." The poet talks about blood that *gushes on the world.* It is not a stream that can be stopped by a styptic agent. John is proclaiming a new world order where the social ills of the world are addressed by people whose own hearts are truly baptized by "the Holy Spirit and fire."

The baptism John describes is an ongoing purification. By virtue of that baptism, each of us is called to conversion and to actions that make Christ present in our world.

For members of my religious congregation, baptism by the Holy Spirit and fire took on a new intensity in 1992, when five of our sisters were martyred in the midst of the civil war in Liberia, West Africa. The blood of our sisters soaked the soil of Liberia and wrote new challenges on the heart of each member of our congregation. The witness of our sisters still impels each of us to look anew at our baptismal commitment.

That's the challenge of today's Gospel message spoken by John the Baptist. Like John's father, Zechariah, we are dumbstruck by the enormity of God's desire to enter the lives of all God's people. We prefer to separate out those whose political views, religious beliefs, and economic practices are different from ours.

Yet all the while, God is waiting to illumine our own lives. Who among us will have the courage of John the Baptist to speak that truth and stand behind our words? It could be that *"Your blood, too, gushes on the world whose fate/ The sun you herald will illuminate."*

Third Sunday of Advent
Matthew 11:2–11

✤ Today we are midway through the season of Advent, a time of in-between—a time of looking back (perhaps with some regrets) on our journey so far and a time of looking forward in hope to the celebration of Christmas.

We're always living between the times, reflecting on what has been and anticipating what will be. Our lives are a careful dance between successes/failures/second thoughts and the reality of waiting for the next thing.

Even though we live in a time of instantaneous communication and microwave ovens for heating our pre-packaged meals, we find in today's Gospel passage we are not so different from John the Baptist. We may communicate in a different manner, and we certainly have a different diet, but John represents for us someone who knew what it means to be an in-between person. He navigated that journey quite well.

While in prison, John asks a question we still ask today. He sends his disciples to Jesus to ask, "Are you the one who is to come, or are we to wait for another?" Jesus responds by sending the disciples back to tell John what they see and hear, essentially that the poor and vulnerable have the good news brought to them.

Then Jesus addresses the crowd—and we can be found among them. "What did you go out into the wilderness to look at?" The wilderness is that in-between place, that place of vulnerability and uncertainty, that place of waiting.

The danger of being in-between is that in our waiting we sometimes don't recognize the One for whom we wait. And so, unconsciously perhaps, we ask, "Are you the one who is to come, or are we to wait for another?"

In the meantime we can languish in the prison of our own blindness and deafness or we can choose to wake up to the unsuspected ways that God is trying to get our attention. Madeleine L'Engle gives us food for thought as we wait.

When will he come
and how will he come
and will there be warnings
and will there be thunders
and rumbles of armies
coming before him
and banners and trumpets
When will he come
and how will he come
and will we be ready

O woe to you people
you sleep through the thunder
you heed not the warnings
the fires and the drownings
the earthquakes and stormings
and ignorant armies
and dark closing on you
the song birds are falling
the sea birds are dying
no fish now are leaping
the children are choking
in air not for breathing
the aged are gasping
with no one to tend them

a bright star has blazed forth
and no one has seen it
and no one has wakened[3]

Fourth Sunday of Advent
Matthew 1:18–24

✤ "There are no small parts. Only small players." This colloquialism has been attributed to a number of people—from the legendary American actress and dancer Ginger Rogers to the Czech novelist, playwright, and poet Milan Kundera. To many it may seem to be a platitude, but the root of the statement is true.

Today's Gospel passage invites us to look at the truth of the statement and reflect on how all of the minor characters in the drama of salvation play their roles. We find that there are no small parts; that each is dependent upon an earlier act of trust by a player who is, indeed, not small.

Today we enter the heart of Joseph, whom Matthew describes as "righteous." The supporting role he plays is essential for Mary's "yes" to come to fulfillment. Matthew's economy of words spares us the angst Joseph must have felt, the terrible dilemma that played out in his mind and heart.

Yet, even in Matthew's abridged version, it is clear that Joseph's love for Mary helps to bring this act of God's story to its dramatic climax. There is another phrase attributed to Milan Kundera that speaks to what stirred in Joseph's heart and ultimately helped him play his part so well: "There is nothing heavier than compassion. Not even one's own pain weighs so heavy as the pain one feels for someone…, pain intensified by the imagination and prolonged by a hundred echoes." What if Joseph lacked that compassion?

And what about the part each of us plays during these last days of dress rehearsal for the celebration of Christmas? God chose to come among the small actors and actresses.

But there are no small parts. And we are small players only if our hearts are small. Perhaps during dress rehearsal we will grow into our role and play it in a new way this Christmas. Consider the part played by one who supported Joseph in this drama, "The Other Grandmother."

What of Joseph's mother?
unstoried and unsung,
did she question the
poignant girl, and
hunt her son's resemblance
in the mysterious child?

Or did she, like others in the story,
Build from doubt a ladder to delight
in a newborn fist and wobbly head?
She didn't guess that God
might clothe himself in skin,
or stir at her whisper, "Grandson." [4]

NOTES

1. Yeats, William Butler, "The Second Coming," in *Immortal Poems of the English Language*, ed. Oscar Williams (New York: Washington Square Press, 1962), 489.
2. Morasztyn, Andrezj, "To St. John the Baptist," in *Divine Inspiration,* ed. Robert Atwan, George Dardess and Peggy Rosenthal (New York: Oxford University Press, 1998), 15.
3. L'Engle, Madeleine, "Advent, 1971," in *The Weather of the Heart,* (Wheaton: Harold Shaw Publishers, 1978), 77.
4. Coffey, Kathy, "The Other Grandmother," in *Hidden Women of the Gospels,* (New York: Crossroads Publishing Co., 1996), 26.

Christmas

Christmas
Luke 2:1-14

✤ There is a story from World War I about British and German soldiers ensconced in their separate foxholes on Flanders Field on Christmas Eve. From one side of the battlefield a soldier spontaneously started singing "Silent Night" in English.

From the other side of the field someone responded by singing the same song in German. Soon both sides were singing in full chorus—together! Putting down their guns, they shook hands with each other and shared photos of loved ones far away. They celebrated Christmas together! Later, they retreated to their separate foxholes. Many could no longer fight against the other side for they realized they were all essentially the same.

There is a mystery in Christmas more persistent than wars and the many differences that seem to separate. World events and international politics cannot halt the birth of an infant whose time has come. God's decree supersedes the decree of the Emperor Augustus.

"While they were there, the time came for her to deliver her child. And she gave birth to her firstborn son and wrapped him in bands of cloth, and laid him in a manger, because there was no place for them in the inn."

Today we celebrate the birth of Jesus. We also celebrate the rebirth of humanity. We celebrate the fact that we can be a people who lay down our arms and sing in harmony. The angel says, "Do not be afraid; for see—I am bringing you good news of great joy for all the people."

Even in those places in the world and in our hearts where joy is swallowed up by sin; we still have to believe God became one of us to transform us, to help us see that in us which is godly.

> In Bethlehem
> a baby's cry
> shatters barriers.
>
> Women, men
> of every creed,
> culture, race
>
> gaze across
> the rubbled walls
> in wonder,
>
> finding every face
> luminous
> with godliness![1]

The goodness in each of us joins the multitude of angels as together we sing, "Glory to God in the highest heaven, and on earth peace among those whom [God] favors."

The Holy Family of Jesus, Mary, and Joseph
Matthew 2:13–15, 19–23

✤ Out of Egypt—again! That's how today's Gospel passage ends, with the Holy Family back in the land of Israel setting up homemaking in a town called Nazareth.

But before that, Joseph is warned in a dream to take his young wife and the child and flee to Egypt. Egypt—how improbable. Surely both Joseph and Mary remembered that Egypt had been a place of bondage for their ancestors. It had been particularly cruel to infants, as Moses could attest. Yet for the infant Jesus, Egypt becomes a place of refuge.

Matthew's account of the flight into Egypt reminds us that we cannot allow ourselves to distance Jesus far beyond the boundaries of humanity. The birth of Jesus that we have just celebrated did not put an end to human tragedy.

Jesus didn't enter a world represented by our sanitized Christmas cards but rather a world of real pain, brokenness, dysfunction, and oppression. Herod represents part of that dark side of humanity. Thomas Merton's poem "The Flight Into Egypt" provides the visuals and sound effects to help bring the message home:

> Through every precinct of the wintry city
> Squadroned iron resounds upon the streets;
> Herod's police
> Make shudder the dark steps of the tenements
> At the business about to be done.
>
> Neither look back upon Thy starry country,
> Nor hear what rumors crowd across the dark
> Where blood runs down those holy walls,
> Nor frame a childish blessing with Thy hand
> Towards that fiery spiral of exulting souls!

Go, Child of God, upon the singing desert,
Where, with eyes of flame,
The roaming lion keeps thy road from harm.[2]

The Holy Family's dramatic escape from Herod's death squads provides a glimpse into the all-too-real world of the condition of immigrants today; especially those who are refugees and exiles, people who are displaced because they have had to flee from the persecution of unjust government, religious intolerance or prejudiced phobias of many kinds. This is where we are challenged beyond the pages of recorded Scripture into the streets of our own cities, towns, and neighborhoods.

Perhaps we have to sojourn a while in the desert with the Holy Family and with those in our society who are displaced, outcast, and the most powerless. What would happen if we made our home there, even briefly?

Merton uses an unexpected image at the end of his poem: *"the singing desert."* For Merton the desert is a place of refuge where one can look out and look within. That is what we are called to do as we reflect on today's Gospel passage, trying to discern how we are to be *"the roaming lion"* who keeps the road from harm for those whom the vulnerable child and his parents represent today.

The child Jesus did not stay long in the desert. In a few verses Matthew will have Jesus present himself for baptism and begin his ministry. Neither can we get too comfortable in our place of reflection, for we also have work to do. Baptism calls us to be a means of sanctuary for those today who come to us out of their own "Egypt."

THE OCTAVE DAY OF CHRISTMAS
The Blessed Virgin Mary, the Mother of God
Luke 2:16-21

✜ In our efficiency, we tend to compartmentalize our lives. Once Christmas Day itself is past, radio stations no longer play Christmas music and even those who believe there is a Christmas season and that "The Twelve Days of Christmas" signifies more than a song are anxious to put away the decorations and get back to the routine of life.

Yet, the Church reminds us that Christmas is not a one-day event but rather an ongoing part of our lives that defies being defined by decorations that come out once a year. So, on this octave of the feast of Christmas and the first day of a new calendar year, we are invited to ponder with Mary, the Mother of God-Become-Human, what the event of Christ's birth means for humanity each and every day.

On this New Year's Day, as we begin another year of our Lord, we are the shepherds that Luke talks about in today's Gospel passage. However, we have to recognize that we do not gather today to worship God-Become-Human amid straw in a manger.

Rather, we gather around the altar where the presence of God transforms us into brothers and sisters as we are reminded by God-Become-Human that each of us bears the image of God.

Somehow it seems easier to find God in a manger than in the people with whom we worship or those we live and work with each day. Maybe that is why we are quick to bring Christmas to a close. Who doesn't feel holy and close to God kneeling at the manger scene? But the child in the manger is all about embracing humanity and challenging us to establish right relationships within human society.

When St. Teresa of Avila, the great mystic, was asked about the heights of prayer she would ask the inquirers how their relationships were going. Each day is Christmas and each day we encounter God in the people we know and love as well as those we find hard to love.

Digby Mackworth Dolben invites us to ponder this mystery:

I

Tell us, tell us, holy shepherds,
What at Bethlehem you saw.—
'Very God of Very God
Asleep amid the straw.'

Tell us, tell us, all ye faithful,
What this morning came to pass
At the awful elevation
In the Canon of the Mass.—

'Very God, of Very God,
By whom the worlds were made,
In silence and in helplessness
Upon the Altar laid.'

Tell us, tell us, wondrous Jesu,
What has drawn Thee from above
To the manger and the Altar.
All the silence answers—Love.

II

Through the roaring streets of London
Thou art passing, hidden Lord,
Uncreated, Consubstantial,
In the seventh Heaven adored.

As of old the ever-Virgin
Through unconscious Bethlehem
Bore thee, not in glad procession,
Jeweled robe and diadem;

Not in pomp and not in power,
Onward to Nativity,
Shrined but in the tabernacle
Of her sweet Virginity.

Still thou goest by in silence,
Still the world cannot receive,
Still the poor and weak and weary
Only, worship and believe.[3]

Luke tells us that the shepherds "made known what had been told them about this child; and all who heard it were amazed at what the shepherds told them." They left the manger "glorifying and praising God for all they had heard and seen."

We leave the altar challenged to "go in peace to love and serve the Lord," the God-Become-Human, the God who *"goest by in silence"* and whom *"Still the world cannot receive."* Dare we, like Mary, ponder it in our hearts and then glorify and praise God as we say, "Thanks be to God."

Second Sunday after Christmas

(If the Epiphany is celebrated on the second Sunday after Christmas, skip to the next meditation.)
John 1:1–18

✦ I give you my word….Sometimes we use that phrase by way of a promise, an assurance of our integrity, a commitment to some action. Only our subsequent actions can verify our word.

Today John the Evangelist reminds us that God gave us the Word, "and the Word was with God, and the Word was God." God has been verifying that promise with actions far beyond our expectations. Yet, even though we would never dare question the integrity of God, we sometimes fail to grasp the wonder of it all: this Word, this Light, this Life came into the world to live with us!

God is not some far-off impersonal deity but a God who truly desires to be with people. God really does want to be a part of and share in our lives. Yes, John tells us, God wants to be with us!

As we listen to the elegant simplicity of John's words in this familiar Gospel passage there is something that lodges in our hearts far beyond what the mind can grasp. As adults we tend to get caught up in mind games and proofs.

But John says, "to all who received him, who believed in his name, he gave power to become children of God." Perhaps that is the secret—"to become children of God." Children have a logic that comes from the heart and can sometimes be so profound.

The theology that undergirds today's reading is anything but simple, but maybe it takes a child to help us find the God who so delights in dwelling in our hearts. Consider "Sharon's Christmas Prayer."

> She was five,
> sure of the facts,
> and recited them
> with slow solemnity,
> convinced every word
> was revelation.
> She said
> they were so poor they had only peanut butter and jelly
> sandwiches to eat
> and they went a long way from home
> without getting lost. The lady rode
> a donkey, the man walked, and the baby
> was inside the lady.
> They had to stay in a stable
> with an ox and an ass (hee-hee)
> but the Three Rich Men found them
> because a star lited the roof.
> Shepherds came and you could
> pet the sheep but not feed them.
> Then the baby was borned.

And do you know who he was?
Her quarter eyes inflated
to silver dollars.
The baby was God.

And she jumped in the air,
whirled round, dove into the sofa,
and buried her head under the cushion
which is the only proper response
to the Good News of the Incarnation.[4]

Our lives may seem like an ongoing Word search, but just for today what would happen if each of the "children of God" could, like Sharon, find our own uninhibited way to celebrate *the Good News of the Incarnation?*" I give you my word…,says God, "And the Word became flesh and lived among us, and we have seen his glory."

The Epiphany of the Lord
Matthew 2:1-12

✤ Perhaps many of us remember our elementary school Christmas pageants reenacted in a similar fashion each year.

The prize parts were Mary and Joseph, usually played by the most photogenic girl and boy in eighth grade. Of course, Jesus might be considered the star; but his part was played by a life-like doll or, if available, some unsuspecting baby who could be counted on to be somewhat quiet under the lights.

The rest of the girls were angels and their mothers were given patterns for wings. The other boys were shepherds—all they needed for costuming was a bathrobe. However, three of the boys would be given special parts with elaborate costumes passed on from pageant to pageant. These were the kings. The major prerequisite for playing a king was to be the right height and girth to fit into the costume.

Surely God smiles on such childish memories where everybody had a part and the scene on stage pretty well depicted the words to

"Silent Night," which everyone sang as parents beamed and focused on their son or daughter, who was the pageant's star regardless of the part.

As adults it is sometimes hard to piece together the memories of Christmases past with today's passage from Matthew's Gospel. Yes, the "kings" arrive but now we are savvy enough to see Herod's treachery and know that life is not as "calm" and "bright" as it may have seemed back in our pageant days.

Hopefully along with the experiences of real life we have gained wisdom and insight into the "kings" who were seekers like ourselves. Today we all play their part in God's drama "[f]or we have observed his star at its rising, and have come to pay him homage." If we have trouble remembering our lines, Irene Zimmerman reminds us that God prefers we speak from the heart.

> What are we who tried so hard
> to keep you far from us,
> addressing you as God Most High,
> Lord, King, and offering gold on gold,
> clouds of incense, myrrh,
> to make of this?
>
> What are we who tried so hard
> to save you from the smell
> of those below the bottom rung
> and now must step around still-steaming
> dung to reach your manger bed
> to make of this?
>
> What are we who tried so hard
> to pick and purchase gifts of royal ilk
> and now see you, despite malodorous
> incense, drafty cold, move toward
> your mother's milk with infant bliss
> to make of this?[5]

Who would have dreamed that God has been right there on stage and off stage with us all along? Kingly robes or bathrobes, golden crowns or homemade wings, we all walk around in the midst of the messiness of humanity—and so does God. What, indeed, are we to make of this?

The Baptism of the Lord
Matthew 3:13–17

✛ One of the prayers spoken *in sotto voce* as part of the preparation of the gifts during the liturgy of the Eucharist might more appropriately be spoken aloud, even proclaimed, on this feast of the baptism of Jesus: "By the mystery of this water and wine may we come to share in the divinity of Christ, who humbled himself to share in our humanity."

Today, despite the protesting of John the Baptist—"I need to be baptized by you, and do you come to me?"—Jesus insists that being baptized by John is the proper and righteous thing to do. By his plunging into the Jordan River, Jesus immerses himself in our humanity. He is willing to stand in solidarity with humanity; to be identified with sinners just like all the others who came to be baptized by John.

Of course, that is what we have been celebrating throughout the Christmas season, but now Jesus' baptism seems to confirm and ritualize this mystery of God-With-Us and thus engages us in a new way.

On the second day of God's creative engagement with the world as recorded in Genesis, God separates the waters above and the waters below by a dome. Like everything else God created, God called it good.

Today's Gospel passage records a new kind of engagement: "And when Jesus had been baptized, just as he came up from the water, suddenly the heavens were opened to him. And a voice from heaven said, 'This is my son, the Beloved, with whom I am well pleased.'" Because this Beloved Son became one of us, we become more than we seem. We become one with the Son and thus we too are the Beloved of God.

From God's perspective, the reality of our sharing in the divinity of Christ happens as suddenly and completely as the heavens were opened at Jesus' baptism. For us, the realization of divinity happens in momentary flashes.

Perhaps that's why the words are spoken *in sotto voce* during the liturgy. Today, however, we try to give voice to the reality as we celebrate not only the baptism of Jesus but our own baptism.

The grace of our baptism actualizes the best in each of us as we celebrate the feast of the baptism of Jesus. For Jesus and for us baptism is more than a ritual; it is a continual invitation to embrace the divine in ourselves and in others. With the poet we loudly proclaim:

> The waters broke
> and Jesus rose—
> the Anointed One.
>
> Clouds tore asunder,
> winged words flew
> to this Noah-Ark,
> this earth was new.
>
> "You are my beloved Son!"
> God spoke
> in glorious thunder.[6]

NOTES

1. Zimmerman, Irene, "Emmanuel: God With Us," in *Incarnation*, (Cambridge: Cowley Publications, 2004), 134.

2. Merton, Thomas, "The Flight into Egypt," in *Selected Poems of Thomas Merton*, (New York: New Directions Publishing Corp., 1967), 4.

3. Dolben, Digby Mackworth, "Flowers for the Altar," in *The Golden Book of Catholic Poetry*, ed. Alfred Noyes (Philadelphia & New York: J. B. Lippincott Company, 1946), 212-213.

4. Shea, John, "Sharon's Christmas Prayer," in *The Hour of the Unexpected*, (Niles, IL: Argus Communications, 1977), 68.

5. Zimmerman, Irene, "Theophany," in *Incarnation*, (Cambridge: Cowley Publications, 2004), 34.

6. Zimmerman, Irene, "Beloved Son," in *Incarnation*, (Cambridge: Cowley Publications, 2004), 43.

Ordinary Time

A NOTE ABOUT ORDINARY TIME

The first week of Ordinary time starts on a Monday; therefore, there is no First Sunday in Ordinary Time.

Ordinary Time is split into two sections by the Lenten and Easter liturgical seasons. On Ash Wednesday, move to the first Lenten reflection (page 97). On the Sunday after Body and Blood of Christ, come back to the Ordinary Time section and pick up on the appropriate Sunday.

The feasts of Pentecost, Most Holy Trinity, and Body and Blood of Christ fall in Ordinary Time; however, because they rely on the date of Easter, they occur on a different Sunday each year. To avoid confusion, we've placed them at the end of the Easter section.

Second Sunday in Ordinary Time

John 1:29–34

✠ Tom Wolfe's book and the movie of the same name, *The Right Stuff*, tell the story of the United States' entry into what was called the Space Age. First Chuck Yeager breaks the sound barrier, the deadly Mach I. Then flyers of all sorts join NASA's space program to compete to be among the elite who would be the U.S. Mercury astronauts, the first from the United States to venture into outer space.

Seven men prove to have the "right stuff" and each has his moment of glory aboard a Mercury space capsule. The courage, discipline and commitment that were required of the Mercury 7 and all subsequent astronauts continue to inspire our admiration and gratitude.

Today's Gospel passage focuses on someone who had the "right stuff" to conquer not outer space but inner space, John the Baptist. It is John of whom Jesus says, "Truly I tell you, among those born of women no one has arisen greater than John the Baptist; yet the least in the kingdom of heaven is greater than he." (Matthew 11:11) The accomplishments of the original astronauts may seem minuscule to us today, but those aboard the international space station know the importance of their contributions. In the same way, those of us who are beginning the long journey through Ordinary Time must recognize the "right stuff" that made John the Baptist the herald of Jesus, the Messiah.

> O blessed Saint John,
> Clean my stained lips,
> That your great deeds
> Pass through my mouth
>   A pure song.

> Lo! the angel, come down from Olympus,
> Tells your father how it will be:
> A great one born, his name,
>   And life history.

> But doubting the heavenly promise,
> He lost his voice,
> Which you regained,
> Fathering your father's speech
>   In your own.

> In that hidden nest of Mary's womb
> You saw a king waiting
> In a bridal chamber.
> Your leap brought both mothers to unfold
>   Secret joys.

Little more than a boy, you sought desert caves,
Fleeing the crowds of town,
That you might not take one stain, speak
    One false word.

A camel covered your shoulders
With his skin.
A goat became a belt for your waist.
You shared their water, their food,
    The locusts and honey.

True, other prophets saw and sang from afar
The approaching light.
But your very forefinger
Picked out
    The Lamb Himself.

Go, circle the immensity of space—
Never was a holier one born than John.
Who but he worthy to bathe the one
    Who bathes the world?

How high you stand above us—
Your soul a peak of snowy whiteness!
Greatest of martyrs,
Who taught the desert to bloom,
    And prince of prophets.

On some heroes they lay thirty crowns,
On others thirty more,
While on your head
They lay three hundred crowns
    Flowing with fruit.

These heavy stones that crush our chest—
Sweep them away, O mighty one!
Smooth and sweeten our road,
And lay it straight to the goal,
    No more retreating.

And do so, not for our sake,
But that the tender savior of the world
Finding us free of fault,
Will joy
    To approach us.

All this in praise of you,
Unity in three.
We beg you spare us,
    Your redeemed.[1]

The poet's heroic depiction of John the Baptist would probably make his sun-darkened face blush. Yet it is a reminder of God's careful preparation to assure that the one who would prepare the way for God's Son had, unquestionably, the "right stuff."

Underlying John's courage, discipline and commitment is a kind of heroic humility. That's today's lesson for all those who explore both outer and inner space as we are launched into this extraordinary time of training called Ordinary Time.

Third Sunday in Ordinary Time
Matthew 4:12–23

✢ There seems to be a giant leap for Jesus and for his followers from the first to the last verse of today's Gospel passage. Matthew begins with what happens when Jesus hears that John has been arrested. Jesus leaves Nazareth and makes his home in Capernaum. He begins preaching and his words at first seem to merely echo those of John the Baptist: "Repent, for the kingdom of heaven has come near."

His arrival by the Sea of Galilee and such preaching seem rather innocuous. It's almost like he is dipping his toe in the water—perhaps testing the religious and political climates and/or himself.

If there is anything tentative about Jesus here, the concern is short-lived. Matthew wastes no time in signaling that Jesus undoubtedly has a firm belief in his own calling and a commitment to move his ministry forward.

Almost immediately he is, figuratively at least, immersed in the water, inviting two sets of brothers to follow him. And "immediately," Matthew tells us, the four honest and hardworking men who until now have been about their ordinary family fishing businesses, leave their boats and nets and follow him.

In today's final verse, Jesus is traveling throughout Galilee teaching in the synagogues, proclaiming the good news of God's reign and curing people of their disease and sickness. The verses move from point to point so quickly there is little time to take in the depth and significance of each movement. We need to replay all of this in our hearts in slow motion to catch up with Jesus and join the queue of those willing to follow him.

Since most of us tend to see the needs of the world through our own personal and local realities, it might help to go to Peter's home and view the scene through his mother-in-law's eyes (and heart).

> My other daughters married well.
> But this one—with his gang of
>   buddies, smelling like the sea,
> carousing as I writhe, feverish.
> Not even the grace or sense
> to quiet down, or eat at John's.
>
> She houses me to stay the
> loneliness (he's often gone).
>   We chat at twilight as
> I braid her hair, stroke
>   the curly tendrils and
> croak her favorite song.

> She worries: he left his nets
> to dog this rabbi—who'll feed
> the family now? I mumble curses
> even as the door opens to cure.
> A touch brushes my hand
> with the coolness of rain.[2]

Maybe discipleship is not about timing after all. Could it be in the readiness to recognize, even as we "mumble curses," God's gentle touch as it "brushes my hand/with the coolness of rain?"

Fourth Sunday in Ordinary Time
Matthew 5:1–12

✤ Praying with the Beatitudes is always a challenge, and most of us struggle with an approach that both justifies and goads us. The easier approach is to pray a bit with each one, reflect on the many ways that we do and don't live its lesson well and then make some firm purpose of amendment.

Admittedly, there is a bit of sadism in this "easier" approach. Another, and perhaps more difficult and certainly more sadistic, approach is to consider the opposite of beatitude, of happiness or blessedness. What happens in our lives when we are not poor in spirit, meek, merciful? Ultimately, it would seem, we are doomed to sadness.

The Beatitudes are a great reminder of the ambivalence that characterizes our lives. Poets have a gift for capturing that reality in a way that other forms of communication tend to "tidy up" or too-quickly categorize. Today we are invited to pray with the Beatitudes using the stream-of-consciousness imagery of César Vallejo.

> There are people so unfortunate that they don't even
> have bodies, hair they have in quantity—
> it lowers by inches the weight of genius;
> their position, upright;

do not seek me, grindstone of oblivion,
they seem to come out of the air, to add up sighs mentally,
to hear sharp blows in their words.

They shed their skins, scratching at the tomb in which they
were born,
and climb up their deaths hour by hour
and fall the length of their icy alphabet to the ground.
Alas for so much! Alas for so little! Alas for them!
Alas in my room, hearing them with eyeglasses!
Alas in my throat when they buy suits!
Alas for my white filth joined in their excrement!

Beloved be the ears of the Joneses,
beloved be those who sit down,
beloved be the stranger and his wife,
our neighbor with sleeves, collars and eyes!

Beloved be he who has bedbugs,
he who wears a torn shoe in the rain,
he who holds a wake with two matches for the corpse of a loaf of
   bread,
he who catches his finger in the door,
he who has no birthdays,
he who lost his shadow in the fire,
he who looks like an animal, he who looks like a parrot,
he who looks like a man, the poor rich,
the simply miserable, the poor poor!

Beloved be
he who hungers
or thirsts, but has no hunger with which to slake his thirst,
and no thirsts that can satisfy all his hungers.
Beloved be he who works by the day, by the month, by the hour,
he who sweats from pain or shame,

he who goes to the movies by the work of his hands,
he who pays with what he lacks,
he who sleeps on his back;
he who no longer remembers his childhood; beloved be
the bald man without a hat,
the just man without thorns,
the thief without roses,
the man who wears a watch and has seen God,
the man who bears an honor and does not weaken!

Beloved be the child who still cries when he falls
and the man who has fallen and cries no longer.

Alas for so much! Alas for so little! Alas for them![3]

The poet's parade of humanity invites us to look in the mirror. Regardless of what we see of both the pride and the pain that line our own faces, today Jesus invites us to find therein the face of God.

In the Beatitudes, Jesus gives us a blueprint for the holiness he came to reveal. The prayer of the Beatitudes begins with careful listening to the beat of our own hearts and ends with finding the face of God both in the mirror and in the world beyond the mirror...

I say more: the just man justices;
Keeps grace: that keeps all his goings graces;
Acts in God's eye what in God's eye he is—
Christ—for Christ plays in ten thousand places,
Lovely in limbs, and lovely in eyes not his
To the Father through the features of men's faces.[4]

Fifth Sunday in Ordinary Time
Matthew 5:13–16

✤ Today our Gospel passage continues Matthew's account of Jesus' Sermon on the Mount. Matthew's compilation of teachings is a call for conversion, a change of heart that will unlock the natural capacities for goodness in Jesus' followers. No doubt, the Beatitudes, which precede today's passage, scared a few folks away. Those who continue to listen hear some very practical applications in four short verses. Jesus uses two common elements of life; but each plays a significant part in the lives of first century and twenty-first century disciples. If we're willing to stay with Jesus and listen to his teachings we have to consider salt and light.

Jesus proclaims, "You are the salt of the earth….You are the light of the world." However, he warns that salt can lose its taste and light can be hidden under a bushel basket. Jesus' disciples cannot be passive, even about the ordinary elements of life. Therefore, we need to think about how salt and light bring out goodness and then apply those qualities to our interactions with others.

Salt doesn't add anything to the quantity of the food we eat, but even those on a salt-free diet reach for a salt substitute of some kind. Light adds nothing to the material composition of the furnishings of a room, yet it allows us to be in proper relationship to those things. Consider a meal without seasoning and a room without light. Jesus' warning is not common or insignificant in any way.

Rather, Jesus challenges his disciples to stir up those elements of Christian life that cannot be taken for granted. It's one thing to recite together the articles of faith in the Creed, but still another to live our faith in such a way that it has an impact and makes a difference in the world. Each of us has to figure out what that means in our individual lives.

> In the world is darkness,
> So we must shine,
> You in your little corner,
> And I in mine.[5]

If we can each be salt in our own corners of the world then there is the chance that our light will spill over into each other's corners and create even more light. We might even be able to give all of those around us a taste of the reign of God.

Sixth Sunday in Ordinary Time
Matthew 5:17–37

✤ Matthew's Gospel account looks "backward" to the Jewish laws and traditions that Jesus fulfills and at the same time looks "forward" to his commissioning of his followers to make disciples of all nations. Before Jesus' followers can embrace their commission they need to understand how that mission squares with the law and the prophets.

As we continue with the Sermon on the Mount, in today's passage Jesus is trying to get his listeners to see beyond the letter of the law and the following of traditional practices; literally, beyond externals to matters of the heart. He is very clear: "[U]nless your righteousness exceeds that of the scribes and Pharisees [those well-versed in the law], you will never enter the kingdom of heaven." Those are strong words and not for the faint-of-heart.

It is much easier to measure the following (and the breaking) of a law or tradition than it is to assess the spirit in which the law or tradition is followed. Instead of a scorecard we need to reverse the process and look at the motivation more than the results.

It's like the game of Jeopardy. In Jeopardy the players are given categorized answers. In order to respond to each "answer," the player must ask a "question." Those who are good at it know a lot of facts, but they also know how to think in reverse. The "answer" is only correct if it is phrased as a "question." Those who make progress toward the reign of God are those who know the law, but they also know how to question the motives that direct their actions.

Jesus challenges his disciples to be self-conscious, not only aware of what we do but why we do it. And as we become more reflective, this self-knowledge should have a positive effect on relationships.

"So when you are offering your gift at the altar, if you remember that your brother or sister has something against you, leave your gift there before the altar and go; first be reconciled to your brother or sister, and then come and offer your gift." Furthermore, since we fall short at times, we become aware we are not in a position to judge the actions of each other, either.

> If you see a tall fellow ahead of a crowd,
> A leader of men, marching fearless and proud,
> And you know of a tale whose mere telling aloud
> Would cause that proud head to in anguish be bowed,
> It's a pretty good thing to forget it.[6]

Sometimes we are the "*tall fellow ahead of a crowd.*" At other times we may feel like an insignificant member of that crowd. Regardless of where we stand, today Jesus says, "Let your word be 'Yes, Yes' or 'No, No'; anything more than this comes from the evil one." Hard words, indeed!

We do well to remember Thomas Becket's words in T.S. Eliot's play, "Murder in the Cathedral," as he faces the tempters who try to sway him from his devotion to the church: "The last temptation is the greatest treason: To do the right deed for the wrong reason."

Seventh Sunday in Ordinary Time
Matthew 5:38–48

✤ One morning on the way to celebrate Eucharist with ordinary people like myself, I heard a touching story on National Public Radio's StoryCorps, a feature that shares the stories of everyday people. The story was about a man whose daughter had been killed by an intruder and his subsequent struggle to deal with the family's devastating loss.

Even though the man was not a proponent of the death penalty, out of his great pain there was a desire to inflict hurt on her killer. In trying to deal with this ambiguity as well as his terrible anguish, the father wanted to learn more about this monster who had inflicted such pain on his daughter and family.

He learned the man had been born in a mental hospital and that years later he and his brother and sister were taken to a swimming pool by their mother, who intended to destroy her children on orders from God. The man and his brother escaped but they had helplessly witnessed the drowning of their little sister.

When the parents of the murdered woman sorted through their pain and understood the pain that had led their daughter's killer down a path of drug addiction, robbery, and eventual murder, they went to the district attorney to ask that the death penalty not be imposed on him.

Later when they had the opportunity to speak as persons who had been affected by the heinous crime, the father looked his daughter's killer in the eyes and said, "I don't hate you, but I hate with all my soul what you did to my daughter." As the man was led from the courtroom with tears streaming from his eyes he said to the parents, "I'm sorry for the pain that I caused you."

The father ended his story by sharing with the listening audience that he felt a weight had been lifted from his own life as he realized he had forgiven his daughter's killer. The story dramatically illustrates the lesson Jesus is trying to teach his disciples in today's Gospel passage.

Most of us do not have a story like the one the forgiving father shared with StoryCorps, but we all have enemies of some sort. How can we possibly love those who harm us? This is such a hard lesson.

The September 11, 2001, terrorist attack on the United States entered the hearts of many of us as a vast collective pain. Patriotism flourished alongside hatred for the unseen enemy who had entered and forever changed our lives.

Individually we learned that a certain ambiguity resided in our own Christian hearts. Jesus' words resounded loudly in our heads and tried to find their way into our hearts: "But I say to you, love your enemies and pray for those who persecute you so that you may be children of your Father in heaven; for he makes his sun rise on the evil and on the good, and sends rain on the righteous and on the unrighteous."

Perhaps the most difficult part of today's lesson is that in order to love our enemies we have to start with checking the condition of our own hearts and finding those places where we need to be transformed. Only then can we change the hearts of our enemies. Jesus says to pray for those enemies. John Greenleaf Whittier offers us "A Prayer."

> Like the publican of old,
> I can only urge the plea,
> "Lord, be merciful to me!"
> Nothing of desert I claim
> Unto me belongeth shame.
>
> Let the lowliest task be mine,
> Grateful, so the work be Thine;
> Let me find the humblest place
> In the shadow of Thy grace:
> Blest to me were any spot
> Where temptation whispers not.
> If there be some weaker one,
> Give me strength to help him on;
> If a blinder soul there be,
> Let me guide him nearer Thee.
> Make my mortal dreams come true
> With the work I fain would do;
> Clothe with life the weak intent,
> Let me be the thing I meant;
> Let me find in Thy employ
> Peace that dearer is than joy;
> Out of self to love be led
> And to heaven acclimated,
> Until all things sweet and good
> Seem my natural habitude.[7]

After hearing the father's story I entered into the liturgy that morning with all of the other faithful everyday Christians; but somehow the Penitential Rite touched the recesses of my heart in a special way. I realized that I will need to repeat this rite over and over *"Until all things sweet and good/Seem my natural habitude."*

Eighth Sunday in Ordinary Time
Matthew 6:24–34

✥ Regardless of our (artificial) social status, our work/ministry, the titles before our names or the initials after, each of us is a servant. The question is, whom do we serve? In today's passage from the Sermon on the Mount, Jesus speaks of the birds of the air and the lilies of the field in a compelling argument for single-heartedly serving one master: God.

Yet, who of us is not tempted to look good in all aspects of our social lives? With the help of Madison Avenue we know the right words to describe our gourmet tastes as we don our designer clothes. We are, after all, self-made people secure in our self-sufficiency!

"Au contraire," says Jesus: "[S]trive first for the kingdom of God and his righteousness, and all these things will be given to you as well." There is nothing inherently wrong with gourmet food, designer clothes or even a certain amount of self-sufficiency. But Jesus is strongly urging us to start first with focusing on the reign of God.

We have to get rid of the trappings of sin that can so deceive us and yield to the truth of our own humanity so in need of redemption. All of us are somewhere along the continuum between being clueless about our own poverty and the ability to embrace with single-hearted purpose God's reign.

One of Jesus' followers who can readily understand how unfocused we can sometimes be is Peter, who often put his designer sandal in his mouth. Today let's join him "In the Servants' Quarters."

Man, you too, aren't you, one of these rough followers
    of the criminal?
All hanging hereabout to gather how he's going to bear
Examination in the hall. She flung disdainful glances on
The shabby figure standing at the fire with others there,
Who warmed them by its flare.

'No indeed, my skipping maiden:
    I know nothing of the trial here,
Or criminal, if so he be.—I chanced to come this way,
And the fire shone out into the dawn,
    and morning airs are cold now;
I, too, was drawn in part by charms I see before me play,
That I see not every day.'

'Ha, ha!' then laughed the constables who also stood to warm
    themselves,
The while another maiden scrutinized his features hard,
As the blaze threw into contrast every line and knot
    that wrinkled them,
Exclaiming, 'Why, last night when he was brought in
    by the guard,
You were with him in the yard!'

'Nay, nay, you teasing wench, I say!
    You know you speak mistakenly,
Cannot a tired pedestrian who has legged it long and far
Here on his way from northern parts,
    engrossed in humble marketings,
Come in and rest awhile, although judicial doings are
Afoot by morning star?'

'O, come, come!' laughed the constables.
'Why, man, you speak the
    dialect

He uses in his answers; you can hear him up the stairs.
So own it. We sha'n't hurt ye. There he's speaking now!
    His syllables
Are those you sound yourself when you are talking unawares,
As this pretty girl declares.'

'And you shudder when his chain clinks!' she rejoined.
    'O yes, I noticed it.
And you winced, too, when those cuffs they gave him
    echoed to us here.
They'll soon be coming down, and you may then have to defend
    yourself
Unless you hold your tongue, or go away and keep you clear
When he's led to judgment near!'

'No! I'll be damned in hell if I know anything about the man!
No single thing about him more than everybody knows!
Must not I even warm my hands but I am charged
    with blasphemies!'...
—His face convulses as the morning cock that moment crows,
And he droops, and turns, and goes.[8]

Only when we can honestly admit we've been with Peter in those servants' quarters can we begin to assess our lives according to Jesus' words today: "No one can serve two masters; for a slave will either hate the one and love the other, or be devoted to the one and despise the other."

Jesus offers more than a challenge. He also offers encouragement: "Therefore do not worry, saying, 'What will we eat?' or 'What will we drink?' or 'What will we wear?'...indeed your heavenly Father knows that you need all these things." The question is, which master will we trust?

Ninth Sunday in Ordinary Time
Matthew 7:21–27

✛ The tension between faith and good works that fueled the Protestant Reformation flames in our hearts as we reflect on today's Gospel passage.

As he concludes the Sermon on the Mount, Jesus addresses both aspects and clearly wants more than lip service from his followers: "Not everyone who says to me, 'Lord, Lord,' will enter the kingdom of heaven, but only the one who does the will of my Father in heaven." Instead of approaching faith and good works as a dichotomy, maybe our primary focus needs to be on the will of God.

As serious followers of Jesus we do try to discern God's will in our lives. In so far as we can know God's will and accept it, the challenge comes in finding God's way of carrying it out. Experience has proven time and again that failing this step results in having things come crashing down all around us.

Each time we start again and pray that God's will truly takes hold in our hearts and in our hands. With Christina Rossetti we pray:

> Use me, God, in Thy great harvest field,
> Which stretcheth far and wide like a wide sea;
> The gatherers are so few; I fear the precious yield
> Will suffer loss. Oh, find a place for me!
> A place where best the strength I have will tell;
> It may be one the older toilers shun;
> Be it wide or narrow place, 'tis well
> So that the work it holds be only done.[9]

Tenth Sunday in Ordinary Time
Matthew 9:9–13

✜ There is a bit of the Pharisee in each of us. It's most at work when we get into comparisons—more accurately, judgments. It happens when we wonder how in the world some unlikely soul can be put in the category of disciple either by himself/herself or by others.

The flip side of being pharisaical is when we fail to be disciples because we feel that God can't possibly expect something from us: What could I possible contribute to the reign of God? Most of the time, however, we spend our lives somewhere between pharisaical pride and false humility.

Today, the call of Matthew challenges each of us to "go and learn what this means: 'I desire mercy, not sacrifice.' For I have come to call not the righteous but sinners." We might start our study of discipleship by praying with John Shea's "A Prayer of Wholehearted Commitment."

> Lord,
> You have the biblical reputation
> of taking people places
> they never wanted to go.
> Witness Jonah
> delivered by whale to Nineveh
> and Habakkuk
> flown by angel to Babylon.
> Also I have heard
> You do not consult.
> Abraham is suddenly ordered from Haran
> and Moses called out of retirement
> for the Egypt assignment.

> Furthermore
> Paul says
> You take a chiropodist's delight
> in Achilles heels,
> spurn eloquence for the stutter,
> and reveal yourself
> in the thorns of the flesh.
> And what was this unpleasantness
> with your Son shortly before
> his appointment at the Right Hand?
> So it is that to You
> my most resounding "yes"
> is a "maybe"
> and it is with one eye on the door
> that I say
> "Behold, Lord, your servant waiteth!"[10]

There's some comfort in joining John Shea and others in praying for wholehearted commitment. Today's account of Matthew's call makes it look like it was easy for him to respond. Jesus walks by his tax booth and says to him, "Follow me." And, we're told, "he got up and followed him." Just like that! Of course, the Pharisees have a problem with this, not because Matthew responded so quickly but because he was not the disciple "type."

Rather than let any past, present, or future disciples get drawn into that judgment of themselves or others as disciple material, Jesus, who knows "my most resounding 'yes'/is a 'maybe'" and that I keep "one eye on the door," assures each of us that he came "to call not the righteous but sinners." The "mercy" Jesus desires starts with our own assessment of our call. Who are we to question the appropriateness of God's call? How can we respond with anything but, "Behold, Lord, your servant waiteth!"

Eleventh Sunday in Ordinary Time
Matthew 9:36–10:8

✢ In today's Gospel passage, Jesus begins to expand his ministry. The need is so great, "the harvest is plentiful, but the laborers are few…" and he can't be everywhere, so he sends out his twelve closest disciples to "cure the sick, raise the dead, cleanse the lepers, cast out demons."

Matthew doesn't tell us how the disciples reacted to his instructions. We have to go to the Acts of the Apostles and the various letters of Peter, John, and Paul and their disciples to know how they really lived up to their commission. Jesus' words are a source of encouragement but we know, as Jesus knew, that they would face many trials as well.

Twenty centuries later, Jesus' heart is still moved to pity over all those who are troubled, marginalized, abandoned. And Jesus is still sending disciples to bring the Good News to those dark corners of our world. The difference is the roster.

The names of the twelve apostles listed by Matthew are replaced by the names of those with whom we live and work, play, and pray. Each of our names are listed, too. We are sent to reach out to those near us as well as those who live continents away. However, most of us are more comfortable reading the Gospel and cheering on the apostles. We don't see our names in such an august list.

Perhaps we make it too complicated. We forget it's often a one-on-one effort to simply do what Jesus did.

Consider the true story of Ron and Nita, two people who live in the same rural area and attend the same church. Ron was involved in a very serious motorcycle accident in front of Nita's home. Nita is a nurse who works each day with mothers and their newborns, both addicted to drugs because of the mothers' use.

Upon hearing the accident, Nita rushed to the roadside to assist. Because she held Ron in the right position as they awaited the ambulance, Ron survived the accident. Ron, of course, will always be grateful to Nita.

But what is most unique about the story is that it was very important to Nita to present Ron with a Bible weeks later as he returned to church. We don't know Nita's motivation or how Ron was touched by her gesture; but as we look more objectively at the exchange, we might conclude that Nita's gift of the gospels to Ron was a mere formality, perhaps a reminder. The real gift is how she lives the gospel day by day.

St. Francis is often quoted as telling his followers, "Preach always. If necessary, use words." It's that simple.

Today Jesus reminds his disciples, both those in the first century and those living in the twenty-first century, that we do what we do through the grace of God. We are chosen and sent. It is God's work, not ours. We have Jesus' words of encouragement wrapped in the words of the poet:

> There is no summit you may not attain,
> No purpose which you may not yet achieve,
> If you will wait serenely and believe.
> Each seeming loss is but a step to'rd gain.
>
> Between the mountain-tops lie vale and plain;
> Let nothing make you question, doubt, or grieve;
> Give only good, and good alone receive;
> And as you welcome joy, so welcome pain.
>
> That which you most desire awaits your word;
> Throw wide the door and bid it enter in.
> Speak, and the strong vibrations shall be stirred;
> Speak, and above earth's loud, unmeaning din
> Your silent declarations shall be heard.
> All things are possible to God's own kin.[11]

Twelfth Sunday in Ordinary Time
Matthew 10:26–33

✟ One of the most popular places for children in a park in downtown St. Louis is a series of fountains that erupt at unexpected times. It is interesting to watch the children's reactions. Some of them stand on the fountainheads seeming to dare the fountain to erupt. Others wait for the eruption and then run through the spray. Still others do the toe test and run away before the soaking can begin.

Even those adults who may secretly wish to be in the midst of the fun can fall into analyzing the developing personalities of the children. We all know children whose play seems to indicate they have no fears.

We also know children whose fears prevent them from joining in the fun. Parents, teachers, and other mentors spend a lot of energy trying to shape those young personalities and help children develop appropriate fears and, hopefully, daring as well.

Jesus addresses fear and daring in today's Gospel passage. He talks about fear in three ways. First, he says not to fear other people's perception of the truth. He knows that in the end *the* truth always prevails. He expects his followers to stand up for the truth even to the point of being more bold in ministry than he seems to be: "What I say to you in the dark, tell in the light; and what you hear whispered, proclaim from the housetops."

Again he says, "Do not fear those who kill the body but cannot kill the soul." Instead, he invites his followers to trust in God's providential care.

Jesus uses two examples of God's care. He talks about a simple sparrow which, in Jesus' time, was food for the poorest people because it sold so cheaply. Yet, a sparrow does not fall to the ground apart from God. And for those who suffer from phalacrophobia (the fear of baldness), Jesus says, "And even the hairs of your head are all counted."

A third time Jesus asserts, "So do not be afraid; you are of more value than many sparrows." Discipleship therefore must be founded on trusting that God's loving care embraces everything from the least to the greatest events in the lives of Jesus' followers.

That kind of trust supports a faith that is personal but not private. It is public because it assumes an identification with Jesus. For Christians, baptism is a public event where the baptized or, in the case of an infant, the parents and godparents, "acknowledge [Jesus] before others."

This Gospel invites us to consider any fears that keep us from discipleship. Jesus seems to indicate that he might tolerate fear that sidesteps danger, but not fear that sidesteps duty. Consider "A Woman's Journey in Discipleship."

Jesus stood waiting for the woman's answer—
not looking past her, not laughing at her.
"Tell me what you need," he repeated, kindly.
"Come, what is it?"

"I don't need anything," she finally answered.
"I'm nothing but a…"
She didn't know how to finish the sentence.
She hung her head. "I'm nothing."

"Ah, you need a name," he said.
I'll give you one: You-Are-Mine."

She thought he meant she was his slave,
so she followed the crowd that was following him.

After three days the people were hungry.
Jesus sat them down in small garden plots
and served fish and bread.
The woman ate with the rest.

When Jesus found her, he asked again,
"Do you know now what you need?"

"Please, Sir, I'm still hungry,"
she answered shyly.

He held out more bread.
"Take! Eat!" he told her.

"Let him put it down," she thought.
"I'm unclean."

It lay in his hands.
"Take it," Jesus urged.

She broke off a piece—
careful not to touch him—
and chewed it slowly, letting the mash
fill her mouth with its goodness.

He watched her swallow it
and asked, "Still hungry?"

She nodded.

"Take more."

When she reached for the bread,
her fingers touched his!
She backed away, frightened,
and awkwardly stumbled.

His right arm encircled her,
hemming her in.
"You-Are-Mine," he said,
"tell me what you need."

"If you please, Sir," she said,
"give me bread like this always."

"Those who follow me
never go hungry,"
he answered her, smiling.
"I am Living Bread."[12]

Authentic discipleship is always a journey. It invites us to replace fear with trust. It invites us to a faith that is daring. Matthew's Gospel challenges us, "Do not be afraid." Today we might dare to feel Jesus' arm encircling us, hemming us in, saying to us, "You-Are-Mine…/tell me what you need." Maybe we'll even stand on the fountainheads waiting to be drenched by the Spirit.

Thirteenth Sunday in Ordinary Time
Matthew 10:37–42

✢ One of life's imponderable questions that children growing up with one or more siblings ask their parents is, "Who do you love the most?" Trying to figure out degrees of love can lead to debates of worth and worthiness that tend to divide.

The wise parent demonstrates it's not a question of more or less but a matter of how they show their love for each child in the many different circumstances of each one's life.

Yet, in today's Gospel passage we do hear that word of comparison: more. Context is important here. Jesus knows his listeners. Extended, closely knit families formed the basis of the society in which he lived.

Outside one's family a person was literally homeless. Jesus knew there would be radical consequences for anyone who truly followed him. To believe in the paradox of the reign of God that Jesus embodied—to dispossess is to possess more—involved risk.

For Jesus, "more" was an invitation to a spirit of self-denial, a willingness to sacrifice everything that comes between his followers and the life that God offers them.

The ideal that Jesus presents means that one loves Jesus in such a way that all other loves—family, spouse, community, friends—assume a secondary importance.

For the follower of Jesus, one's true family has to embrace all those whom God loves. It involves hospitality, righteousness and simple gestures of love like sharing a cup of cold water.

Ultimately, all other loves are enriched, purified and empowered to grow when we truly make God the primary love of our life. In the meantime, we keep sorting through all the degrees of love in our lives and questioning who loves whom best.

Today's Gospel passage invites us to dispense with all the ranking and search our hearts and lives to find our true Love.

> God came to my house and asked for charity.
>   And I fell on my knees and
>   cried, "Beloved,
>
>   what may I
> give?"
>
> "Just love," He said.
>   "Just love."[13]

Fourteenth Sunday in Ordinary Time
Matthew 11:25–30

✤ After a series of skirmishes with the "wise" teachers of his day and the news that John the Baptist is imprisoned, Jesus tries to center himself in today's Gospel passage. He prays, "I thank you, Father, Lord of heaven and earth, because you have hidden these things from the wise and the intelligent and have revealed them to infants."

This seems to be a reversal of popular wisdom. Wanting to be wise ourselves, we have to ask, "What are those hidden things, that truth, to which Jesus is referring?"

It helps to situate our own lives within the scene. Who among us does not know what it means to have a "heavy" day? The demands of family, work, community, health issues, financial challenges, and so much more can leave us feeling weary.

That's when it helps to do what Jesus did: consider the children. There is an energy and an innate wisdom in children that lets them live in the present moment without judgment. This seems to be founded on a sense of dependence and trust. As adults we get caught up in the many responsibilities (real and unreal) that we claim and which claim us.

It's easy to forget that God is ultimately in charge. Today Jesus is inviting us to embrace this truth, to feel God's embrace. He uses the image of a yoke.

Most of us are not familiar with yokes, although we may have seen pictures of oxen yoked together or people using a yoke to carry buckets of water on their shoulders.

A yoke offers a way to balance a burden between draft animals or across one's shoulders. The key lies in balancing the distribution of weight. That is what Jesus does for himself and what he invites us to do as well. "Take my yoke upon you, and learn from me; for I am gentle and humble of heart." He is offering to share those burdens that weigh us down.

We experience those flashes of dependence and trust and each time hope we will remember the gift of that yoke the next time our weariness threatens to overcome our joy and sense of child-like freedom. The fourteenth-century Italian poet Petrarch verbalizes it for us:

> I tire so beneath this ancient load
> of sin and bitter use: I pray
> I will not falter on the way
> and fall into the hands of my foe.
>
> True, once a great friend eased it so
> in his ineffable courtesy;
> but then he hastened off so quickly
> that soon I had no friend to behold.

Even so, his voice rings from above:
"O you who labor, here is the way;
Come to me, if the way stands clear."

What grace, what love, O what fate
will grant me wings as of a dove,
that I might rest and fly from here?[14]

In Jesus' imagery today, burdens can become blessings. We all have burdens, but Jesus says bearing any burden is possible when the weight is shared. He is inviting us to trust that God is part of the journey with us. But Jesus also says, "learn from me." He is challenging us to learn how to be yoke bearers with others. Each of us can name people who have borne our pain and helped us carry the crosses that have been part of our lives. We, in turn, must learn the compassion that can lighten the burdens of others. "What grace, what love, O what fate."

Fifteenth Sunday in Ordinary Time
Matthew 13:1–23

✣ During the excavations of ancient Egyptian tombs, grains of wheat over 4,000 years old were found among the mummies. These grains were planted and actually germinated.

Whether seed is 4,000 years old or packaged for the current year, a key factor in its germination is the condition of the soil. The skilled sower knows what needs to be done to assure that the seed is placed in good soil.

Jesus uses the image of a sower to teach his followers about preparing our hearts to receive his Word. He provides a kind of examination of conscience.

Each of us has to apply the parable to our own *Sitz im Leben*, "situation in life." Is the soil of my heart hard-packed like an earthen path, making me self-sufficient and impervious to the movement of God's love within? Is the soil of my heart shallow, allowing me to be superficial in my response to God's call? Is the soil of my heart contaminated with thorns, distracting me from focusing on God's will in my life?

Answering these questions is not easy. However, Jesus is enabling each of us to identify those things that need to be corrected in order to fully use the gifts that God has given. He says, "Blessed are your eyes, for they see, and your ears, for they hear."

The wisdom of the thirteenth-century Afghan poet Rúmí both challenges and encourages us to prepare our hearts well:

God hath placed a ladder before us: we must climb it,
step by step.
You have feet: why pretend to be lame? You have hands:
why conceal the fingers that grip?
Freewill is the endeavour to thank God for His Beneficence;
your necessitarianism denies that Beneficence.
Thanksgiving for the power of acting freely gives you more
power to thank Him; necessitarianism takes away what
God hath given.
The brigands are on the road: do not sleep until you see
the gate and the threshold!
If you put trust in God, trust Him with your work! Sow
the seed, then rely upon the Almighty![15]

Passivity is not an option for one who wants to be among Jesus' disciples "who indeed bears fruit and yields, in one case a hundredfold, in another sixty, and in another thirty."

Sixteenth Sunday in Ordinary Time
Matthew 13:24–43

✣ Physicists have spent decades, even entire careers, searching for the elusive Higgs boson, also known as the "God particle." This special subatomic particle allows all of the other particles of the universe to have mass and come together to form, basically, everything that's around us.

Scientists believe the Higgs boson could contain the very essence, or at least the mechanism, of existence itself. Without the so-called "God particle," atoms theoretically have no integrity. Therefore, there would be no chemical bonding, no solids or liquids. So, understanding the "God particle" is essentially understanding how matter becomes and remains matter.

Jesus' frequent use of agricultural images in his parables suggests he had a basic understanding, as did most of the people of his time, of simple biological concepts. Consider his references to planting good and bad seeds and to the ability of a small mustard seed to become a tree and of yeast to leaven flour.

Perhaps he knew something about physics, too. When he explains to his disciples about the good seed, he is talking about a kind of "God particle." It is that essence of goodness, of God, within human beings that makes "the righteous…shine like the sun" in God's reign.

Finding the "God particle" Jesus talks about can take decades. Maybe that's why Matthew included the mustard seed and yeast parables in the midst of the story about good and bad seed. Good things take time to develop and rise up within us. The poet Edmond Gore Alexander Holmes articulates the journey for us:

Hemmed in by petty thoughts and petty things,
Intent on toys and trifles all my years,
Pleased by life's gauds, pained by its pricks and stings,
Swayed by ignoble hopes, ignoble fears;
Threading life's tangled maze without life's clue,
Busy with means, yet heedless of their ends,

Lost to all sense of what is real and true,
Blind to the goal to which all Nature tends:--
Such is my surface self: but deep beneath,
A mighty actor on a world-wide stage,
Crowned with all knowledge, lord of life and death,
Sure of my aim, sure of my heritage,--
I – the true self – live on, in self's despite,
That 'life profound' whose darkness is God's light.[16]

Perhaps as each of us becomes more "sure of my aim, sure of my heritage" we'll know that "God particle" within ourselves, "that 'life profound' whose darkness is God's light," and we will be able to plant good seed among the weeds.

Seventeenth Sunday in Ordinary Time
Matthew 13:44-52

✤ Some people have a real talent for wrapping packages. Others may not wrap the packages very well but the gift inside is always a wonderful surprise. Our God, the God of abundance, always sends wonderful gifts; but sometimes the packaging is not what our human eyes recognize as spectacular.

Jesus' parables about the reign of God are like a wrapped gift. You might have to peel away the layers of meaning but in the end you always have in hand a wonderful gift if you persevere in the unwrapping.

Today's Gospel passage invites us to unwrap three such stories. Jesus tells us the reign of God is like a treasure someone found hidden in a field.

We don't know if the field is a vacant lot overgrown with weeds or something a bit more esthetically appealing, but we do know the person sold everything in order to purchase the whole field. Likewise, the very observant merchant in the second story sells all he has to purchase one pearl of great value.

Finally, Jesus says the reign of God is like a net that is thrown into the sea and which catches fish of every kind. The good fish are sorted out from the bad. Perseverance in the midst of evil yields the best gift of all for those who are good.

Those who recognize the reign of God in the midst of their everyday lives have a special sensitivity to everything and everyone around them. Their lives are marked with joy regardless of their circumstances. Consider Elizabeth Barrett Browning's definition of life. It seems to have a lot to say about the reign of God.

> Each creature holds an insular point in space;
> Yet what man stirs a finger, breathes a sound,
> But all the multitudinous beings round
> In all the countless worlds with time and place
> For their conditions, down to the central base,
> Thrill, haply, in vibration and rebound.
> Life answering life across the vast profound,
> In full antiphony, by a common grace?
> I think this sudden joyaunce which illumes
> A child's mouth sleeping, unaware may run
> From some soul newly loosened from earth's tombs:
> I think this passionate sigh, which half-begun
> I stifle back, may reach and stir the plumes
> Of God's calm angel standing in the sun.[17]

The poet reminds us that once our minds and hearts unwrap that gift marked "reign of God," we find there "Life answering life across the vast profound." We find that the reign of God brings all people and things together; we need only to have keen eyes that find treasures hidden in fields and pearls of great price in the midst of a vast net that encompasses all.

There's a story about a new pastor and his wife who discovered the reign of God in a very unusual way. Their first ministry opportunity was to reopen a rundown church in Brooklyn. For months they worked hard to repair, plaster and paint the church so that they could open the doors to the congregation on Christmas Eve.

All was progressing nicely until a storm on December 19 revealed a leaky roof which caused a large area of plaster to fall off of the sanctuary wall behind the pulpit.

The pastor, resigned to postponing the reopening of the church, passed a flea market on his way home that night. He saw there a beautiful handmade ivory colored tablecloth exquisitely crocheted and with a cross embroidered in the center. It was just the right size to cover the hole in the sanctuary.

As he excitedly headed back to the church he met an older woman who had just missed her bus. He invited her to wait in the warm church until the next bus arrived. The woman sat in a pew and paid no attention to the pastor, who was hanging the tablecloth as a tapestry in front of the hole.

Looking up, she discovered the tablecloth and asked the pastor where he got it. She asked him to check to see if the initials EBG were crocheted into the right corner. They were. She had embroidered those initials on the tablecloth when she made it 35 years ago in Austria.

She explained that, during the war, when the Nazis came, she was forced to leave her home and her husband. He was later captured and imprisoned and she never saw him again. She would not take the tablecloth back but she did accept the pastor's offer of a ride home to the other side of Staten Island.

After a wonderful Christmas Eve service, the pastor noticed an older man continued to sit in the church as everyone else went home. The older man asked the pastor where he got the tapestry on the sanctuary wall because it was identical to a tablecloth his wife had made many years ago in Austria.

The pastor smiled and asked the man if he would allow him to take him for a little ride. They drove to Staten Island to the same house where the pastor had taken the woman just days earlier. He helped the old man climb the stairs to the woman's apartment.

That night, once again, the pastor unwrapped the gift of the reign of God. "Life answering life across the vast profound."

Eighteenth Sunday in Ordinary Time
Matthew 14:13-21

✤ The gospel writers don't portray Jesus as a hermit or a religious recluse. Even when he tried to go to a deserted place by himself following the death of John the Baptist, the crowds followed him.

"When he went ashore, he saw a great crowd; and he had compassion on them and cured their sick." It seems that wherever Jesus goes he is in the midst of the people. Occasionally those people are religious leaders who dog him, trying to catch him in some nuance of their law. Others are disciples or would-be disciples.

But in today's Gospel passage, as in so many others, the majority of the people who make up that crowd are ordinary people. They follow Jesus with different motives and different needs. Some are alienated by their sin or marginalized by their social status. Others are sick, homeless, or destitute. Some feel the burden of Roman rule or suffer from the onus of taxes. Among them are those who want to hear about the establishment of the reign of God. Some are simply curious.

Regardless of each person's motivation or need, Jesus never seems annoyed with the ordinary people. He never tells them they are poor because they are lazy or that they deserve to be ostracized because of their lifestyle.

He doesn't connect their sickness with sin—their own or that of others. Nor does he say they should be deprived of public services because they somehow don't belong. The Gospel simply says, "...he had compassion on them."

Jesus knows that the common people who follow him are not all what we would call saints, holy men and women. He also knows that some of them follow him for less than spiritual reasons. He knows many are victims of unjust political and religious leaders. Others just never had a chance to break from the poverty that oppresses them.

Clearly, saint or sinner, rich or poor, Jesus makes no distinctions when he orders the crowd to sit down on the grass. What he does do is treat everyone as someone who counts.

Regardless of the hunger which brought each person to that

deserted place that day and kept them there well into the evening, each will leave knowing that Jesus understands all hungers and no one is insignificant.

Kathy Coffey has a poem which invites us to reflect on the effects of the miracle of the loaves and fish on the ordinary people who are present. The speaker in the poem is Raissa, the mother of the young boy who had the five loaves and two fish, as noted in John's account (John 6:9).

> I wasn't counted, but I ate my unofficial fill.
> I played my part in seeding this desert,
>   channeling the silvery cascade of fish.
> Who do you think brought the baskets?
>
> The children just chewed, smiles crumb-smudged.
> Unimpressed by murmurings of miracle or gourmet reviews,
>   they swallowed a lavish memory, extravagance
>   overflowing the rationed plates of other days.
>
>   Another hunger soothed by the reverence in hands
> touching loaves as if they were ivory
> blessing bread as if an empress dined
>   lifting us like crystal goblets to each other's lips.
>
>   Afterward, gummed crusts gathered with care
> bent grass imprinted with our sheen.
>   We left plucky as a people dared, feisty, fueled,
>   yeasty, dangerous. Almost as if we count.[18]

The ordinary people for whom Matthew wrote this Gospel story were no different from the participants in that drama. And neither are we. We, too, live in an age of alienation, marginalization, displacement, poverty, and oppression.

Jesus may not literally invite us to sit in the grass and share bread and fish, but he does invite us take another look at our lives and those of the ordinary people with whom we rub shoulders throughout the day. Would that we each had such "a lavish memory" of being fed by Jesus in deserted places and in the midst of great crowds. Then perhaps we would each know that our hungers are satisfied by Jesus.

Nineteenth Sunday in Ordinary Time
Matthew 14:22–33

✤ People who never seem to make a misstep, who always seem to succeed, who always know the right things to say and do are sometimes described as "walking on water." At least in the perception of some of those around them, their extraordinary insights and abilities help them to always get it right.

Among those who are perceived to "walk on water," there are those who recognize their talents as God-given; and perhaps only those who are closest to them know the struggles that underpin the gifts which they share. There are others who think they "walk on water" and, well, the adage, "pride cometh before the fall" comes to mind.

Those who belong in the former category of water-walkers are the focus of today's Gospel passage, and Peter is their patron saint. In this scene, Jesus' disciples are in a boat making the passage to the other side of the lake while Jesus stays in the mountains to pray. Their boat is far from land and battered by wind and waves.

After a stressful night the disciples see what appears to them to be a ghost coming toward them on the water and they cry out in fear. "But immediately Jesus spoke to them and said, 'Take heart, it is I; do not be afraid.'" He speaks to them of faith and fear.

Faith and fear. The words are more than alliterative. They form the bedrock of the true water-walkers that we are all called to be. We spend much of our lives rowing into the wind. The ambiguities of life shake our safe boats and challenge our faith.

There is an inverse correlation between faith and fear, and it can take us a lifetime of struggle to understand that and step through our fears so we can ultimately walk across the water into the loving arms of God. Perhaps the question to ask about Peter in today's Gospel is not, "Would Peter have succeeded in walking on the water if he had a bit more faith?"

Rather, the question might be, "What shred of faith prompted Peter to get out of the boat and start walking toward Jesus?" That's the journey each of us is on. Denise Levertov invites us to consider that journey in "Poetics of Faith."

> 'Straight to the point'
> can ricochet,
> unconvincing.
> Circumlocution, analogy,
> parable's ambiguities, provide
> context, stepping-stones.
>
> Most of the time. And then
>
> the lightning power
> amidst these indirections,
> of plain
> unheralded miracle!
> For example,
> as if forgetting
> to prepare them, He simply
> walks on water
> toward them, casually—
> and impetuous Peter, empowered,
> jumps from the boat and rushes
> on wave-tip to meet Him—
> a few steps, anyway—
> (till it occurs to him,
> 'I can't, this is preposterous'
> and Jesus has to grab him,
> tumble his weight
> back over the gunwale.)

> Sustaining those light and swift
> steps was more than Peter
> could manage. Still,
> years later,
> his toes and insteps, just before sleep,
> would remember their passage.[19]

Our struggle with faith is activated by the fears, both recognized and unrecognized, that mark our days: fear of offending, of not having the right answers, of where the world is going. Letting go of those fears is a confirmation of faith. Day by day, like Peter, we make "a few steps, anyway—/(till it occurs to [us],/'I can't, this is preposterous.'" Jesus tumbles us "back over the gunwale." And we begin again to touch into the faith stirring deep inside that lets us own our fears and suspend the laws of physics and of human nature and allow Jesus to invite us outside our safe boats once more.

Today's Gospel passage ends with the disciples in the boat professing, "Truly you are the Son of God." As we pray our Profession of Faith, we join Peter, who shows us it's not enough to know Jesus walked on water; we also need to step outside our comfort zones and believe there is life outside the boat. As we live that Profession of Faith, we grow like Peter into the realization and firm belief that, just before we enter into that sleep where we will awaken into life everlasting, our "toes and insteps../[will] remember their passage."

Twentieth Sunday in Ordinary Time
Matthew 15:21-28

✤ What parent who has held a sick child has not bartered with God? Even when speaking in hyperbole, "I'll do anything...," the parent's heart is focused only on the child. In today's Gospel passage, we meet a woman who knows that anguish. Matthew tells us that her daughter is "tormented by a demon." We don't know what that broad first-century label actually means. Perhaps the daughter suffered from epilepsy or mental illness of some kind. The illness itself is not important. What is important is the woman's persistent love and Jesus' response to her.

It's easy to get caught up in the external circumstances of the story. In addition to the fact that the petitioner is a woman, she is a Canaanite. In the popular prejudices of the first century, she is second class on two counts. The fact that she approaches Jesus is clearly unthinkable. We also can get distracted by Jesus' reaction to her. His cool reception seems out of character for "the healer" who has scorned popular perceptions about laws and worthiness.

Since Matthew recorded the story decades later, it is impossible to catch all of the nuances of the verbal exchange between the two. As it is written, the interchange takes the form of a debate. In a debate, there is typically a winner and a loser. However, in this encounter between two great debaters there are two winners. The woman gets what she came for: "And her daughter was healed instantly." But Jesus wins something, too, in terms of his own self-understanding. Her challenge to him seems to mature and expand his concept of messiahship. His words, "Woman, great is your faith!" might express an "aha" moment in his ever-deepening wisdom and understanding of the reign of God. Perhaps the debaters bring mutual healing as well.

> Jesus planned their day of R & R
> carefully. He led his followers to a far
> seashore to avoid the usual needy crowd.
> But there a Canaanite woman came with loud
> persistent shout
> until he had to listen, had to hear her out.
>
> When finally he understood her urgent matter
> (She wanted him to heal her dying daughter!),
> he told her there was nothing he could do
> for her: she wasn't family, wasn't a Jew.
> It was to them alone that he was sent.
> Doggedly, she squelched that argument

and would not quit until he saw a wider mission:
Would his good God not set aside a tired
tradition
dividing race and class and creeds
to tend an innocent child's needs?
"Family" includes the dogs, not only those who
    sit
at table. He saw her point, marveled at her wit,

and did a human-Godly thing—
he gave her dying child a spring.[20]

Twenty-first Sunday in Ordinary Time
Matthew 16:13–20

✣ Keys play a very important role in our lives. Most of us need keys
to get into our homes and places of business. Beyond the ordinary
functionality of keys, there are those who attach great importance
to keys.

Some think a massive key ring weighed down by all kinds of
keys is a measure of authority and importance. Others may view
the same collection of keys as an oppressive burden. Depending on
how one has viewed the display of multiple keys, the introduction
of numeric codes such as those on padlocks and car doors has affected the importance of keys.

And beyond keys and codes that give us physical entry, we now
carry in our heads multiple passwords that give us entry into com-
puter programs, voice mail and a whole cadre of other important
functions.

Ultimately, keys, codes, and passwords all serve the same
purposes: they give us a certain amount of power and at least the
semblance of security. Who wouldn't be flattered by the award of
the symbolic key to a city?

What teenager doesn't look forward to the possession of car
keys? Who isn't tempted to be a bit smug about knowing codes

and passwords that get one into all kinds of important cyberspace places that others may not even know exist?

In today's Gospel passage it is Peter who knows the code word that gets him the most important set of keys any follower of Christ could ever dream of carrying.

When Jesus asks the big question, "But who do you say that I am?" it is Peter who knows the password: "You are the Messiah, the Son of the living God." Knowing the right answer got Peter the keys to heaven! Who wouldn't be caught up in the power and security of that set of keys?

The Chinese poet Zhang Xingyao celebrates with Peter and at the same time lends perspective to the scene.

> How wonderful was Peter,
> a sage who was a great cornerstone for the Teaching.
> A fisherman who was commanded,
> to leave his family and follow the Lord.
> His love for the Lord was so filled with reverence,
> that he was a great wave hurling onward.
> A massive mountain of shining light,
> he swore an oath to totally commit his time,
> and sincerely believed in complete self-cultivation.
> He underwent all sorts of worldly suffering,
> and the spiritual light illumined his mind.
> He was a sage who spread the teaching throughout a wide area.
> He elevated the Teaching to a supreme position.
> He lived five lives in only one lifetime,
> and sacrificed his life in hurling himself against Satan.
> He had the keys to open Heaven's blessings.[21]

Xingyao's reflection on Peter invites us to consider our own attachment to the power that can be wielded with keys, codes and passwords vis-à-vis the reality of Peter's life. Jesus is essentially giving Peter the key to the city of God.

Most recipients of the key to an earthly city are so honored because of commitments and actions that merit the admiration of others. At this particular part of Matthew's Gospel, Peter seems to be given the key before he actually earns it.

However, Matthew's contemporaries know, and so do we, that Peter will undergo "all sorts of worldly suffering" to earn the trust that key represents and that ultimately he will give his life in "hurling himself against Satan."

It will not take Peter long to learn that the privilege of sitting in the driver's seat must be accompanied by responsibility. The poet calls Peter "a sage" but we know he will have to learn from many mistakes before he becomes proficient in "binding" and "loosing" from God's perspective.

Jesus final word in today's Gospel passage is to all of his disciples. He says "not to tell anyone that he was the Messiah." Like Peter, a disciple needs to grow into the privilege of proclamation.

Whatever gives us a sense of power and security is effective only in so far as it is treated as a gift we are given to be shared responsibly for the sake of the reign of God. Today we can use the symbolism of the keys, codes and passwords that form the fabric of our external lives to open our hearts and minds to formulate our response to "but who do you say that I am." Perhaps we might even find "the keys to open heaven's blessings."

Twenty-second Sunday in Ordinary Time
Matthew 16:21-27

✣ In 1917, the U.S. Congress approved a measure allowing families with loved ones in the military to display a Blue Star Service flag on a front window of their homes. This practice continues today. The symbol represents the family's support for their son or daughter, brother or sister, and by its display invites passersby to be supportive as well.

In today's Gospel passage, Peter and the other disciples are offered the opportunity to embrace the full meaning of Jesus' message—his impending suffering, death and (perhaps hardest to understand) rising to new life.

Their heads and hearts must have been spinning with incredulity as he spoke about losing life in order to find it, gaining the whole world and forfeiting life in the process, and then his ultimate words: "Truly I tell you, there are some standing here who will not taste death before they see the Son of Man coming in his kingdom."

Even after all those months of listening to Jesus, watching him interact tenderly with the most vulnerable and perhaps secretly applauding as he challenged those who put law before life, the disciples would still have trouble connecting the reign of God with losing life in order to truly live. Peter, hearing only the words about suffering and death, speaks for all of them: "God forbid it, Lord! This must never happen to you."

Peter's heart has not yet been stretched far enough to take in the expansiveness of God's love. We know he won't learn this too quickly, either. Today Jesus calls Peter "a stumbling block." Later, after Jesus is arrested, Peter will stumble himself as he denies the very person who offers him life. It is only after the risen Jesus appears to him and the others on the beach that Peter is able to get back up.

It helps to understand today's passage from Matthew if we fast-forward to the account of Jesus' suffering and death. While Jesus is falsely accused as he stands on trial before Caiaphas the high priest and the council, Peter is telling his own lies as he denies any knowledge of Jesus. Today, built over the remains of Caiaphas' palace, is a church called St. Peter in Gallicanto, St. Peter of the Cock Crow. Outside the church is a statue of St. Peter which helps us image Peter as he stood in the courtyard with his back to his friend's trial proceedings. Thomas Merton's poem, "The House of Caiaphas," describes the scene:

> Somewhere, inside the wintry colonnade,
> Stands, like a churchdoor statue, God's Apostle,
> Good St. Peter, by the brazier,
> With his back turned to the trial.

As scared and violent as flocks of birds of prey,
The testimonies of the holy beggars
Fly from the stones, and scatter in the windy shadows.

The accusations of the holy judge
Rise, in succession, dignified as rockets,
Soar out of silence to their towering explosions
And, with their meteors, raid the earth.

And the gates of night fall shut with the clangor of arms.

The crafty eyes of witnesses, set free to riot,
Now shine as sharp as needles at the carved Apostle's mantle.
Voices begin to rise, like water, in the colonnade;
Fingers accuse him like a herd of cattle.

Then the Apostle, white as marble, weak as tin
Cries out upon the crowd:
And, no less artificial than the radios of his voice,
He flees into the freezing night.

And all the constellations vanish out of heaven
With a glassy cry;
Cocks crow as sharp as steel in the terrible, clear east,

And the gates of night fall shut with the thunder of
Massbells.[22]

The poem jolts us beyond the typical statues of the papal Peter
back to the reality of the exchange between Peter and Jesus in today's Gospel passage. Peter, stumbling block that he is, will know
the cross that Jesus promises. He'll stumble a few times but in the
end he too will stand before Caiaphas and speak boldly in the name
of Jesus Christ of Nazareth (see Acts 4).

Blue Star Service flags speak in the name of freedom. Behind
the display lives a family whose ordinary life is marked with the

possibilities of the price of freedom. The poet reminds us that our human betrayals of each other locally and nationally "Rise, in succession, dignified as rockets,/Soar out of silence to their towering explosions/And, with their meteors, raid the earth" as "Cocks crow as sharp as steel in the terrible, clear east…"

Today's Gospel passage is not to be taken lightly. Like Peter, we have to grow into a firm commitment. "If any want to become my followers, let them deny themselves and take up their cross and follow me."

Twenty-third Sunday in Ordinary Time
Matthew 18:15–20

✤ …*First Do No Harm* is a 1997 made-for-TV movie which tells the true story of Lori Reimuller, whose son is diagnosed with epilepsy. After the efforts of the medical profession fail to help her son, Lori finds an alternative treatment called the Ketogenic Diet.

The plot of the movie revolves around her battle with her son's doctor who wants to discuss only the treatment options that he knows and favors. The title of the movie is from a phrase usually attributed to the Hippocratic Oath taken by doctors who swear to practice medicine ethically.

Lori's battle with the medical establishment is not unlike the battles that can sometimes play out among faith communities. By virtue of our baptism we all promise to practice our faith based on the code of ethics lived by Jesus.

However, any one of us can get blinded by routine preferences, by our own selfish motives, by the evil that entices us each day. Jesus understands all this. After all, he did keep searching for the lost sheep. So in today's Gospel passage, Jesus commissions us to point out to each other any faults we observe in another. This is no small commission. Not only is it hard to confront another, we must be careful to "first, do no harm."

It's easier to judge the actions of another from afar. Even physically close, we can't see into the other's heart. Yet, in order to "point out the fault" we have to try to place ourselves in the heart of the other to discover what is preventing the goodness of the other from being engaged.

It takes genuine love to do this well. Most of us are more comfortable with the kind of intellectual argument that characterizes civil courts. Fraternal correction as Jesus outlines it in today's Gospel requires a love for another which will risk rejection and a fractured relationship in order to help the other. It also must be accompanied by forgiveness.

In the process of correcting another member of the church we might also wonder if we need to be brought before others and accused of our own sinfulness "by the evidence of two or three witnesses." Each day we sit in the borderland between correcting others and needing to be corrected by others. The poet Tagore describes "The Borderland."

> I saw, in the twilight of flagging consciousness,
> My body floating down an ink-black stream
> With its mass of feelings, with its varied emotion,
> With its many-colored life-long store of memories,
> With its flutesong. And as it drifted on and on
> Its outlines dimmed; and among familiar tree-shaded
> Villages on the banks, the sounds of evening
> Worship grew faint, doors were closed, lamps
> Were covered, boats were moored to the ghāts. Crossings
> From either side of the stream stopped; night thickened;
> From the forest-branches fading birdsong offered
> Self-sacrifice to a huge silence.
> Dark formlessness settled over all diversity
> Of land and water. As shadow, as particles, my body
> Fused with endless night. I came to rest
> At the altar of the stars. Alone, amazed, I stared
> Upwards with hands clasped and said: 'Sun, you have removed
> Your rays: show now your loveliest, kindliest form
> That I may see the Person who dwells in me as in you.'[23]

On the borderland between righteousness and sinfulness we each pray "That I may see the Person who dwells in me as in you." To find the God who dwells in each of us makes it easier to address that which is not of God and, in any confrontation, to "first, do no harm."

Twenty-fourth Sunday in Ordinary Time
Matthew 18:21–35

✛ "Forgive us our trespasses as we forgive those who trespass against us." How many times have we prayed those words that accompany sincere sentiments of praise—"Hallowed be thy name"—and trust that God will give us "our daily bread?" Each time we pray the Lord's Prayer we not only express praise of and trust in God, we commit ourselves to be people of forgiveness.

So, forgiveness should be second nature to us. However, there are times when we find ourselves identifying with the "wicked slave" as well as with the merciful king who forgives the slave's debts in today's Gospel passage.

Today, if we can own the infinite Love that forgives us over and over, maybe we can find that forgiveness which we profess so often. Rabia of Basra, the Islamic mystic and poet who grew up in what is present-day Iraq, can help us find a way into forgiveness:

It acts like love—music—
it reaches toward the face, touches it, and tries to let you know
His promise: that all will be OK.

It acts like love—music, and,
tells the feet, "You do not have to be so burdened."

My body is covered with wounds
this world made,

but I still longed to kiss Him, even when God said,

> "Could you also kiss the hand that caused
> each scar,
>
> for you will not find me until
> you do."
>
> It does that—music—helps us
> to forgive.[24]

We strive with our finite language to name the mystery that is a merciful God. Rabia suggests that music "reaches toward the face, touches it, and tries to let you know/His promise: that all will be OK."

And, in "The Mourning Bride" the playwright/poet, William Congreve, says, "Music has charms to soothe a savage breast." Music does soothe us while it stirs us and puts noble feelings in us. Maybe today we need to pray the Gospel with music, letting it wash over us and cleanse us. Then we might be able to embrace Jesus' exhortation to forgiveness, "Not seven times, but, I tell you, seventy-seven times."

As we reflect with music on the gift of forgiveness, we might think about the fact that the ability to sing and to appreciate music is one of the last faculties that a person with dementia loses. Maybe our gentle God knows it takes a lifetime to learn forgiveness. Today's Gospel offers us another opportunity to get ourselves in tune with the heart of God, remembering that *music—helps us/to forgive.*"

Twenty-fifth Sunday in Ordinary Time
Matthew 20:1–16

✣ It really doesn't matter where it came from or who said it first, but most of us are quite familiar with the idiom, "Pull yourself up by your bootstraps."

The world of corporations and of those who are socially and financially well-positioned freely use the phrase to exhort those who sit (idly, from their perspective) on the lower rungs of society. Even without "position," our competitive nature likes to measure everything. Fairness is measured by *quid pro quo*. There should be no "free rides." So, wherever we find ourselves on the "fairness in the workplace" continuum, today's Gospel passage is disconcerting.

Jesus is not addressing evil people. He's talking to ordinary folks, challenging good people to be better. In a hymn from a treatise on Easter by Hippolytus of Rome we find a reflection on the higher standard to which Jesus calls his disciples:

Do you honor God? Do you love him
—here's the very feast for your pleasure.
Are you his servant, knowing his wishes?
—be glad with your Master, share his rejoicing.
Are you worn down with the labour of fasting?
—now is the time of your payment.

Have you been working since early morning?
—now you will be paid what is fair.
Have you been here since the third hour?
—you can be thankful, you will be pleased.

If you came at the sixth hour,
you may approach without fearing:
you will suffer no loss.
Did you linger till the ninth hour?
—come forward without hesitation.
What though you came at the eleventh hour?
—have no fear; it is not too late.

God is a generous Sovereign,
treating the last to come as he treats the first arrival.
He allows all his workmen to rest—
those who began at the eleventh hour,
those who have worked from the first.
He is kind to the late-comer
and sees to the needs of the early,

gives to the one and gives to the other:
honors the deed and praises the motive.

Join, then, all of you, join in our Master's rejoicing.
You who were the first to come, you who came after,
come and collect now your wages.
Rich men and poor men, sing and dance together.
You that are hard on yourselves, you that are easy,
honor this day.
You that have fasted and you that have not,
make merry today.

The meal is ready: come and enjoy it.
The calf is a fat one: you will not go hungry away.
There's a kindness for all to partake of and kindness to spare.

Away with pleading of poverty:
the kingdom belongs to us all.
Away with bewailing of failings:
forgiveness has come from the grave.
Away with your fears of dying:
the death of our Saviour has freed us from fear.
Death played the master: he has mastered death...
The world below had scarcely known him in the flesh
when he rose and left it plunged in bitter mourning.

Isaias knew it would be so.
The world of shadows mourned, he cried, when it met you,
mourned at its bringing low, wept at its deluding.

The shadows seized a body and found it was God;
they reached for earth and what they held was heaven;
they took what they could see: it was what no one sees.
Where is death's goad? Where is shadow's victory?

Christ is risen: the world below is in ruins.
Christ is risen: the spirits of evil are fallen.
Christ is risen: the angels of God are rejoicing.
Christ is risen: the tombs are void of their dead.
Christ has indeed arisen from the dead,
the first of the sleepers.

Glory and power are his for ever and ever. Amen.[25]

The poet puts all efforts at social stratifying in the perspective of the resurrection. Literally and figuratively, we are invited to another plane. Today we try to put on the mind and heart of God. We might also try to remember all the times we were the ones who got the "free ride." If we must measure, let's count our blessings.

Twenty-sixth Sunday in Ordinary Time
Matthew 21:28–32

✚ How does one earn another's trust? It is seldom won by words. Rather, it is by our actions that others come to know who we truly are. Our words are only as good as the deeds that accompany them.

What parent, or for that matter any leader or mentor of others, has not been caught in the trap of having to say, "Do what I say, not what I do?" Talk is cheap, as the second son in today's Gospel passage illustrates.

Jesus uses the story of the two sons to teach a lesson to the chief priest and elders. He cuts to the quick. These leaders of the people assume that their positions have earned them the trust and respect of the people. They have no qualms about telling others what to do.

In their righteousness they find it difficult to accept the conversion of tax collectors and prostitutes, whose actions they have consistently condemned. Yet it is their own conversion that Jesus is addressing.

This story is for us as well. Words…actions…trust. What are

others to believe about us? Sit with the poet Rabia's camels as you
ponder:

> Once I heard two camels talking,
>   they were complaining about all the weight they had to carry
>   when they crossed the desert,
>
> and they were especially peeved about the new camel whose
> only
>   load was the master's young daughter who would often
>   pet the camel and even sing to it sweet songs,
>
>   while they had to often feel the whip of men
> and listen to them tell crude stories of romantic exploits.
>
> An older camel was overhearing the chat, as I was, and spoke
> saying,
>   "You know, it is our habit to bite when we are grouchy and
> just yesterday I saw you snap at that man who whipped you—
>   maybe you shouldn't bite; maybe the master has two
>   daughters who sing and pet,
>   and although this may be stretching things a bit
>   I am reminded of some words of wisdom
> I have been trying to work in
>   somewhere,
>   for days:
>
>   Those who are trusted by others
> God trusts."[26]

Twenty-seventh Sunday in Ordinary Time
Matthew 21:33–43

✣ Every one of the fifty states that make up the United States has at least one vineyard. Many of the smaller vineyards are family-owned and operated. Others, like the one in today's Gospel passage, are owned by absentee landlords who carefully plan the vineyard and then leave the operation to tenants.

Jesus' parable today invites us to consider the tenants in relation to the landowner. There is an accountability that underlies the parable. That is where we are to focus. The tenants in the story got greedy and wanted the inheritance for themselves. We don't usually see ourselves as that kind of tenant. We'd like to think that we are good stewards who would recognize the landowner's slaves, or certainly his son.

Yet, we do have to acknowledge Jesus' words: "I tell you, the kingdom of God will be taken away from you and given to a people that produces the fruits of the kingdom." We are not among those who lose their lease. If we were, we would not be struggling to understand this parable and apply it to our own lives. For us the question becomes, "What kind of vintage do we have to give back to God?" Have we followed the landowner's formula or do we keep insisting on our own?

Perhaps a reversal of the landowner/tenant relationship will help each of us answer the question.

The Father
knocks at my door
seeking a home for his son:

Rent is cheap, I say.

I don't want to rent. I want to buy, says God.

I'm not sure I want to sell,
but you might come in to look around.

I think I will, says God.

I might let you have a room or two.

I like it, says God. I'll take the two.
  You might decide to give me more some day.
I can wait, says God.

I'd like to give you more,
    but it's a bit difficult. I need some space for me.

I know, says God, but I'll wait. I like what I see.

Hm, maybe I can let you have another room.
I really don't need that much.

Thanks, says God. I'll take it. I like what I see.

I'd like to give you the whole house
but I'm not sure—

Think on it, says God. I wouldn't put you out.
Your house would be mine and my son would live in it.
  You'd have more space than you'd ever had before.

I don't understand at all.

I know, says God, but I can't tell you about that.
You'll have to discover it for yourself.
  That can only happen if you let him have the whole house.
A bit risky, I say.

Yes, says God, but try me.

I'm not sure—
I'll let you know.

I can wait, says God. I like what I see.[27]

Vineyard tours and wine-tastings are quite common. We learn that careful pruning produces good vintage. Today we are asked to learn the fine art of pruning. Our "landowner"—God—will patiently wait for the finished product.

Twenty-eighth Sunday in Ordinary Time
Matthew 22:1–14

✤ Sometimes in order to move forward, one has to look backward. To understand the parable Jesus tells in today's Gospel passage and embrace its meaning for each of us right now, it helps to look over the paths we've already trod. Each of us is a pilgrim—a person who journeys a long distance to some sacred place as an act of religious devotion.

As we make our way to that sacred place, that heavenly banquet, we are always looking for markers to keep us on the right path. Reflecting on the journey to this point gives us a clearer sense of the next right moves. Our point of entry is Yeats' poem, "When You Are Old."

When you are old and gray and full of sleep,
And nodding by the fire, take down this book,
And slowly read, and dream of the soft look
Your eyes had once, and of their shadows deep.

How many loved your moments of glad grace,
And loved your beauty with love false or true;
But one man loved the pilgrim soul in you,
And loved the sorrows of your changing face.

> And bending down beside the glowing bars
> Murmur, a little sadly, how love fled
> And paced upon the mountains overhead
> And hid his face amid a crowd of stars.[28]

Today each of us can take down the book of our lives and reflect on all the invitations that God has sent us. Some of them came with gilded edges and we failed to respond because, like the people in the Gospel passage, we had things to protect and work to do. Some invitations we simply tore up.

Other invitations seemed less formal and we found ourselves among both the good and the bad as the wedding hall filled with guests. Uncomfortable with sharing the banquet with all the "street people," we were careful not to identify with the mob.

In the midst of all those missed opportunities, however, we remember that "one man loved the pilgrim soul in you,/And loved the sorrows of your changing face." Our God also reminds us of all the times we did respond well.

All the times we came to Eucharist and recognized the faces of our brothers and sisters. All the times we heeded the dismissal challenge at the end of the Eucharist, "Go in peace to love and serve the Lord." All the times we responded affirmatively to the RSVP enclosed with the invitation. That's why we are still pilgrims.

We close the book, pray that we find the God who "hid his face amid a crowd of stars" and carefully open the next envelope: "God requests the honor of your presence…"

Twenty-ninth Sunday in Ordinary Time
Matthew 22:15–21

✤ "The job of the newspaper is to comfort the afflicted and afflict the comfortable." Most of us who are familiar with the latter part of this sentence are not aware of its origin a century ago by Finley Peter Dunne, a journalist who wrote in the voice and persona of an Irishman named "Mr. Dooley."

He is commenting on the power of the media to influence society. Today Jesus asks each of us to reflect on all the factors that influence our actions.

The context of today's Gospel passage is the ongoing confrontation between Jesus and the Pharisees. The glib words of the Pharisees drip with honey as they extol Jesus' sense of fairness, his sincerity and truth. All the while their intent is to trap him.

The Pharisees live to protect the law. Jesus recognizes their malice and even calls them hypocrites. Before we put our hands on our hips and stand smugly behind Jesus in this confrontation, we all have to admit there's a bit of Pharisee in each of us, too. It's easier to follow civil and religious law than to form our consciences according to God's law of love.

Law is so clearly spelled out and sometimes leaves little for interpretation. We often forget that law follows life and that laws were created to give life to a society.

Individually and collectively we've all been under the influence of laws that are later acknowledged to be ill-conceived and actually wrong. The civil rights movement of the 1960s was a major wake-up call for everyone who lived through that time of great unrest and call to conscience. Consider Merton's "And the Children of Birmingham."

> And the children of Birmingham
> Walked into the story
> Of Grandma's pointed teeth
> ("Better to love you with")
> Reasonable citizens

Rose to exhort them all:
"Return at once to schools of friendship.
Buy in stores of love and law."
(And tales were told
Of man's best friend, the Law.)

And the children of Birmingham
Walked in the shadow
Of Grandma's devil
Smack up against
The singing wall.
Fire and water
Poured over everyone:
"Hymns were extreme,
So there could be no pardon!"

And old Grandma
Began the lesson
Of everybody's skin,
Everybody's fun:
"Liberty may bite
An irresponsible race
Forever singing,"
Grandma said,
"Forever making love:
Look at all the children!"

(And tales were told
Of man's best friend, the Law.)

And the children of Birmingham
Walked into the fury
Of Grandma's hug:
Her friendly cells
("Better to love you with.")

Her friendly officers
And "dooms of love."

Laws had a very long day
And all were weary.

But what the children did that time
Gave their town
A name to be remembered!

(And tales were told
Of man's best friend, the Law.)[29]

Merton gives us a powerful reminder of what law without love can do. In his confrontation with the Pharisees Jesus doesn't repudiate the law. He says, "Give therefore to the emperor the things that are the emperor's, and to God the things that are God's."

Like the Pharisees, we're left to sort through our hidden agendas and challenged to act out of the appropriate authority. Perhaps today Mr. Dooley is asking each of us to consider whether Jesus' words comfort us because we are among the afflicted or afflict us because we are among the comfortable.

Thirtieth Sunday in Ordinary Time
Matthew 22:34–40

✠ "All you need is love." Anyone familiar with the music of the Beatles probably tended to sing, or at least hum the melody, of this simple sentence even as you read it. The Beatles first sang this memorable song in 1967 via satellite to an audience of four hundred million people in twenty-six countries.

But, as today's Gospel passage reminds us, the concept was certainly not new. Jesus said it to an, albeit smaller, audience centuries before: "You shall love the Lord your God with all your heart, and with all your soul, and with all your mind....You shall love your neighbor as yourself. On these two commandments hang all the law and the prophets."

Like the Beatles, Jesus was also speaking about something that his listeners would not necessarily have found original. The first commandment to love God absolutely was recited by devout Jews every morning and evening. It was the great *Shema Yisrael*—"Hear, O Israel: The Lord is our God, the Lord alone."—found in the book of Deuteronomy (6:5). The second commandment was familiar as well. "You shall love your neighbor as yourself" is also from the cherished Torah—from the book of Leviticus (19:18). What was unique to the ears of Jesus' listeners was the fact that Jesus put the two commandments together.

The Pharisee lawyer who posed the question, "Teacher, which commandment in the law is the greatest?" probably got more than he bargained for in Jesus' response. So did all of the other listeners, both the sincere followers and the cynics alike. Jesus told them, and today he tells us, that all that is needed is love: love of God, neighbor and self.

"All you need is love." The sentence is simple but living the reality is not. It helps to reflect on the fact that we are first loved by God. If we can truly embrace that fact, then the rest should follow.

Why should I wish to see God better than this day?
I see something of God each hour of the twenty-four, and each
    moment then,
In the faces of men and women I see God and in my own face in
    the glass,
I see letters from God dropped in the street, and every one is
signed
    by God's name.[30]

God doesn't need communications satellites to tell the world about love. God has you and me and all the people we meet today as we spend the day picking up love letters from God and singing, "All you need is love. All you need is love. All you need is love."

Thirty-first Sunday in Ordinary Time
Matthew 23:1–12

✤ Sometimes when we think we are doing everything right, we are, in the final analysis, so very wrong. Most of the time we try to do the right thing; to lead good and upright lives, following all the rules and avoiding anything that others would consider scandalous. What could be so wrong with that?

The scribes and Pharisees that Jesus describes in today's Gospel passage might ask that very question. As Jesus pokes holes in their inflated righteousness we smugly cheer him on because we see the inconsistency and not-so-subtle insincerity of their actions. Perhaps we can even name their twenty-first-century counterparts. Yet, while Jesus is talking about the scribes and Pharisees, it is his followers that he is addressing.

There's a certain discomfort in hearing Jesus' words today because they challenge us to look beneath our actions to the very core of our being. We're not bad people but each of us has to examine our relationship with God and own those areas where we get in the way of letting God simply be God in our lives. Perhaps we try too hard, analyze too much, get too comfortable in our service of others. The poet Adelaide Anne Proctor gives us something to reflect on:

I

The Monk was preaching: strong his earnest word;
From the abundance of his heart he spoke,
And the flame spread,—in every soul that heard
Sorrow and love and good resolve awoke:—
The poor lay Brother, ignorant and old,
Thanked God that he had heard such words of gold.

II

'Still let the glory, Lord, be thine alone,'—
So prayed the Monk, his heart absorbed in praise:

Thine be the glory: if my hands have sown
The harvest ripened in Thy mercy's rays,
It is Thy blessing, Lord, that made my word
Bring light and love to every soul that heard.

III

'O Lord, I thank thee that my feeble strength
Has been so blest; that sinful hearts and cold
Were melted at my pleading,—knew at length
How sweet Thy service and how safe Thy fold:
While souls that loved Thee saw before them rise
Still holier heights of loving sacrifice.'

IV

So prayed the Monk: when suddenly he heard
An Angel speaking thus: 'Know, O my Son,
The words had all been vain, but hearts were stirred,
And saints were edified, and sinners won,
By his, the poor lay Brother's humble aid
Who sat upon the pulpit stair and prayed.'[31]

Thirty-second Sunday in Ordinary Time
Matthew 25:1–13

✤ The first Christians for whom Matthew wrote his Gospel some-times needed a pep talk; for after waiting for the return of Christ, nothing seemed to be happening. We, too, have days and weeks like that. Fidelity can be burdensome. So today's parable about the bridesmaids is for twenty-first-century Christians as well as for those who lived in the first century.

All of us are bridesmaids who wait with the bride for the arrival of the bridegroom so we can go through the streets with our torches and engage the entire village in the wedding procession.

In the parable, Jesus doesn't focus on the bride and groom, the traditional stars of the show. Instead, he talks about those who wait. What restaurant owner focuses on the wait staff—those we typically call waiters and waitresses? In the restaurant or any kind of service business, the customer is number one. But Jesus asks us to focus on being part of the wait staff. And so we are.

Our experience as customers can tell us a lot about the difference between those who wait well and those who don't. We know there is a difference between productive and nonproductive activity and between genuine attentiveness and mere functional listening. Those who wait successfully bring heart and accountability to their service. They actually seem to take pleasure in waiting. They know the waiting itself is an important part of any worthwhile enterprise.

The same is true of the bridesmaids in Jesus' parable. The wise ones know how to wait well. Their wisdom is not in accurate calculations about measures of oil and the time of the bridegroom's arrival but in knowing how to wait well.

They are not functionaries but people who know the Light that they carry. The foolish bridesmaids, on the other hand, are like people who know doctrine but never know God; people who own a Bible but do not own or allow themselves to be owned by the God of the Bible. Half measures are not enough. Today Jesus is telling us that our faith has to go deeper. Knowledge about God is worthless unless it leads to a surrender of self to God.

> As swimmers dare
>   to lie face to the sky
>   and water bears them,
>   as hawks rest upon air
>   and air sustains them,
>   so would I learn to attain
> freefall, and float
>   into Creator Spirit's deep embrace,
>   knowing no effort earns
>   that all-surrounding grace.[32]

Jesus has much more than a good supply of oil in mind when he tells his followers to "keep awake therefore, for you know neither the day nor the hour." It's not about knowing times and measures but about having an expectant attitude of faith.

It's a kind of fidelity that knows how to wait attentively, knowing that giving one's hand to God is a kind of free fall into the unknown. It is when we are thus waiting that the bridegroom arrives and we *"learn to attain/freefall, and float/into Creator Spirit's deep embrace."*

Thirty-third Sunday in Ordinary Time
Matthew 25:14–30

✤ In the movie *The Year of Living Dangerously,* based on a novel of the same name by Christopher Koch, the main character, Guy Hamilton, has some risky choices to make.

As an Australian journalist in Indonesia during the overthrow of President Sukano, Hamilton gets caught in all of the intrigue which such a setting implies. He befriends his local contact and photographer, Billy Kwan, who in turn introduces him to Jill Bryant, an assistant at the British Embassy.

In the course of the action the three fall in and out of friendship and love. Hamilton has to make some choices that ultimately involve his own personal safety and his very life. What complicates the choices is his relationship with the other characters.

The parable in today's Gospel reading is about risks and choices too. Today's passage is the third in a series of parables Jesus uses to illustrate to his disciples what he means by "watch." We've heard the story many times before: A man goes on a journey and entrusts his property to his slaves.

What is entrusted to each slave is a specific number of talents. At first blush, twenty-first-century disciples think of a talent as a personal ability, a kind of natural gift. Jesus' first-century disciples would think of a particular amount of money—a weight of silver worth about $1,000. The parable invites us to look deeper than personal abilities and money.

Consider the fact that the talents given are the property of the man who is the master in the story. Matthew is clear to say "his property." The talents are given to persons, in this case slaves, who have a relationship with the man. They are distributed not as personal abilities or money but on the basis of each person's natural ability. Each person is to invest the talent or talents received so as to benefit the master, not the recipient.

In the movie cited above, Guy Hamilton's life ultimately rests in his ability to invest his love and trust in someone besides himself.

In the story of the talents, Jesus invites his disciples to take the risk of investing their love and trust in someone besides themselves—himself. The very life of each disciple in the first and twenty-first centuries and all of the centuries in between involves the same kind of risk. Each disciple is called to look for opportunities to invest the master's talents.

Those opportunities are the moments of decision, the risky choices that we are invited to invest ourselves in. Whether the choice involves a decision about job or ministry, a life partner, a particular stance on an issue, or a life/death healthcare matter, as a disciple none of us can let himself or herself get in the way.

"Will this choice give me what I want or will it make it possible for Jesus to do what he wants through me?" We spend our lives, not just *The Year of Living Dangerously*, trying to be faithful in investing God's talents.

Yet, today the One whose very being is Love challenges us to risk making that investment. Alcuin, an eighth-century disciple who distinguished himself as a schoolmaster called by Charlemagne to reform the King's Palace school and as abbot of St. Martin's at Tours, reflected on the investment of talents in a poem written to Abelhard, Archbishop of Canterbury:

> Brief is our life, now in the midst of the years,
> And death with silent footfall draweth near.
>   His dreaded fingers are upon the gates,
>   And entering in, takes all thou hast.
> Look forward to that day, and to that unloved hour
> That when Christ come from heaven

He find the father of the house still watching,
  And then thou shalt be blessed.
Happy the day when thou shalt hear the voice
Of thy gentle Judge, and for thy toil rejoicing:
  'Come, my most faithful servant, enter in
  The kingdom of the Father everlasting.'
That day, remember me, and say:
  'O Christ most gentle,
  Have mercy on a poor man, Alcuin.'
And now,
Beside the shore of the sail-winged sea
I wait the coming of God's silent dawn.
Do thou help this my journey with thy prayer.
  I ask this, with a devoted heart.[33]

I hope each of us finds ourselves like Alcuin, investing our talents well. Let's watch together and pray for that for each other *"with a devoted heart."*

Feast of Christ the King
Matthew 25:31–46

✤ On the way to celebrate the Eucharist on the feast of Christ the King, I reflected on the contrast between kingship perceived in earthly terms with all its superficial glory and separateness and the genuine inclusiveness Christ brought to us.

Outside the church, blankets are spread in the midst of protective shrubbery, and folded cardboard "homes" lean against the ramp which is intended to make the building accessible to all. The steps into the church are steep, the distance equivalent to another floor or level, and are somewhat precarious due to the loss of the handrails which have perhaps long since been sold for food or drugs by someone who calls this part of the city "home."

Inside the church the faithful have ample opportunity to reflect on another aspect of the communion of saints as multiple statues and murals depict the lives of familiar people the Church has named holy. These saints reside at still another level, hovering closer to the ceiling than to the floor. Embraced by this holy hall of fame, the faith community tries to bridge the gap with canned and boxed food carried in procession and placed on the ornate altar at the back of the sanctuary.

The passage from Matthew's Gospel for this Feast of Christ the King verbalizes the contrast and puts us in the middle with two choices and the consequences of each: "Truly I tell you, just as you did it to one of the least of these who are members of my family, you did it to me....Truly I tell you, just as you did not do it to one of the least of these, you did not do it to me."

The choice is right or left, separation or inclusion; but most of us live with the fact that, in spite of our best efforts, we often fall short. So we gather for the Eucharist to own the struggle and search together for ways to make the reign of God present. The reality of the challenge is not new:

> On a night filled with stars,
> Christ broke through our defenses,
> disarming us with infant cries.
> Kings from foreign countries
> came to give him homage
> but left again without a trace.
>
> Years went by. Hearing nothing,
> we regrouped, returned to battles.
> He reappeared in the countryside,
> recruiting the peasants
> and sabotaging our strategies
> by commands to love the enemy.
>
> We infiltrated his company,
> set him up as "King of the Jews"
> and nailed him for it on execution hill.

Now, rumors whisper,
he has eastered back behind our lines
to plot a reign of peace.[34]

Suspended between grime-filled blankets and dusty statues, we celebrate Christ our King.

NOTES

1. Paulus Diaconus, "Ut Queant" in Divine Inspiration edited by Robert Atwan, George Dardess and Peggy Rosenthal (New York: Oxford University Press, 1998), 65–67.
2. Coffey, Kathy, "Sara, Peter's Mother-in-Law" in *Hidden Women of the Gospels* (New York: The Crossroads Publishing Company, 1996), 52.
3. Vallejo, César, "Stumble Between Two Stars," in *Divine Inspiration* edited by Robert Atwan, George Dardess and Peggy Rosenthal (New York: Oxford University Press, 1998), 287–288.
4. Hopkins, Gerard Manley, from No. 34, in *Poems and Prose of Gerard Manley Hopkins* edited by W.H. Gardner (Baltimore: Penguin Books, 1953), 51.
5. Anonymous, "Shining," in *Inspiring Poems* compiled by C.B. Eavey (Grand Rapids: Zondervan Publishing House, 1970), 20.
6. Anonymous, "Forget It," in *Inspiring Poems* compiled by C.B. Eavey (Grand Rapids: Zondervan Publishing House, 1970), 54.
7. Whittier, John Greenleaf, "A Prayer," in *Inspiring Poems* compiled by C.B. Eavey (Grand Rapids: Zondervan Publishing House, 1970), 49.
8. Hardy, Thomas, "In the Servants' Quarters," in *Divine Inspiration* edited by Robert Atwan, George Dardess and Peggy Rosenthal (New York: Oxford University Press, 1998), 416–417.
9. Rossetti, Christina, "Use Me, God," in *Inspiring Poems* compiled by C.B. Eavey (Grand Rapids: Zondervan Publishing House, 1970), 49.

10. Shea, John, "A Prayer for Wholehearted Commitment," in *The Hour of the Unexpected"* (Niles, IL: Argus Communications, 1977), 90.
11. Wilcox, Ella Wheeler, "God's Kin," in *Simple Graces* edited by Gretchen L. Schwenker and Mathew J. Kessler, C.Ss.R. (Liguori: Liguori Publications, 2008), 45.
12. Zimmerman, Irene, "A Woman's Journey in Discipleship," in *Incarnation* (Cambridge:Cowley Publications, 2004), 127–129.
13. Francis of Assisi, "He Asked for Charity," in *Love Poems from God,* trans. Daniel Ladinsky (New York: Penguin Compass, 2002), 33.
14. Petrarca, Francesco, "I Tire So Beneath This Ancient Load," trans. Jack Roberts, in *Divine Inspiration* edited by Robert Atwan, George Dardess and Peggy Rosenthal (New York: Oxford University Press, 1998), 323.
15. Rúmí, "Faith and Works," in *Poetry of the Spirit* edited by Alan Jacobs (London: Watkins Publishing, 2002), 69.
16. Holmes, Edmond Gore Alexander, "La Vie Profunde," in *Poetry of the Spirit* edited by Alan Jacobs (London: Watkins Publishing, 2002), 371.
17. Browning, Elizabeth Barrett, "Life," in *Poetry of the Spirit* edited by Alan Jacobs (London: Watkins Publishing, 2002), 282–283.
18. Coffey, Kathy, "—and Me, Raissa," in *Hidden Women of the Gospels* (New York: The Crossroads Publishing Company, 1996), 66.
19. Levertov, Denise, "Poetics of Faith," in *The Stream and the Sapphire* (New York: New Directions Books, 1997), 37–38.
20. Zimmerman, Irene, "Expanding the Mission," in *Incarnation* (Cambridge: Cowley Publications, 2004), 79.
21. Xingyao, Zhang, "How Wonderful Was Peter," in *The Forgotten Christians of Hangzhou* translated by D.F. Mungello (University of Hawaii Press, 1994). Reprinted in *Divine Inspiration* edited by Robert Atwan, George Dardess and Peggy Rosenthal (New York: Oxford University Press, 1998), 215.

22. Merton, Thomas, "The House of Caiphas," in *Selected Poems of Thomas Merton* (New York: New Directions Publishing Corp., 1967), 30–31.

23. Tagore, Rabindranath, "The Borderland–9," in *Rabindranath Tagore: Selected Poems* (New York: Penguin Books, 1985), 107.

24. Rabia, "It Acts Like Love," in *Love Poems From God* trans. Daniel Ladinsky (New York: Penguin Compass, 2002), 21.

25. Hippolytus of Rome, "Do You Honor God?" in *Divine Inspiration* edited by Robert Atwan, George Dardess and Peggy Rosenthal (New York: Oxford University Press, 1998), 263–264.

26. Rabia, "Trying to Work In," in *Love Poems From God* trans. Daniel Ladinsky (New York: Penguin Compass, 2002), 17.

27. Halask, Margaret, "Covenant" in *Life Through a Poet's Eyes* compiled by David L. Fleming, SJ (St. Louis: Review for Religious, 1999), 9.

28. Yeats, William Butler, "When You Are Old," in *Timeless Voices* compiled by Virginia Larrain (Berkeley: Celestial Arts, 1978), 57.

29. Merton, Thomas, "And the Children of Birmingham," in *Selected Poems of Thomas Merton* (New York: New Directions Publishing Corp., 1967), 116–117.

30. Whitman, Walt, "To See God," in *Poetry of the Spirit* edited by Alan Jacobs (London: Watkins Publishing, 2002), 321.

31. Proctor, Adelaide Anne, "A Legend," in *The Golden Book of Catholic Poetry* edited by Alfred Noyes (Philadelphia & New York: J.B. Lippincott Company, 1946), 206.

32. Levertov, Denise, "The Avowal," in *The Stream and the Sapphire* (New York: New Directions Books, 1997), 6.

33. Alcuin, "Brief is Our Life," trans. Helen Waddell, in *Divine Inspiration* edited by Robert Atwan, George Dardess and Peggy Rosenthal (New York: Oxford University Press, 1998), 279.

34. Zimmerman, Irene, "A Different Kind of King," in *Incarnation* (Cambridge: Cowley Publications, 2004), 135.

Lent

Ash Wednesday
Matthew 6:1–6;16–18

✤ Today we receive ashes in a communal setting; yet each of us approaches the minister alone because no one else can own what is in the recesses of our hearts. No doubt, there are those standing in line who may judge by our daily interactions the state of our hearts—and admittedly we do the same to them—but when Jesus issues the call to give alms, pray, and fast, he makes it very personal:

"When you give alms, do not let your left hand know what your right hand is doing, so that your alms may be done in secret." "Whenever you pray, go into your room and shut the door and pray to your Father who is in secret." "When you fast, put oil on your head and wash your face, so that your fasting may be seen not by others but by your Father who is in secret."

While almsgiving, prayer and fasting hopefully will have a positive effect on our local and world communities, we each enter this journey alone. Lent is an invitation to renew our relationship with God. It is a challenge to transformation that has to be deeply interior if it is to bring about a spiritual change. Lent starts within the confines of an intimate relationship with God: Creator, Redeemer, Sanctifier. In the imagery of the poet, this journey, if it is genuine, is truly a "Wounding."

Intrusive God,
you wound me most exquisitely,
piercing deep
until my heart trembles
and I grow faint,
losing all consciousness
of time, place,
color, shape,
sound or sense.

I swoon
in your embrace.
The world spins
and I know nothing
beyond the spreading wound
which is both ecstasy
and pain.

God, you have left your mark
on me,
have branded me
with your love,
burned me with your spirit,
lanced me
with your presence.

Transfixed,
I cry out—
not for release
but for a wounding so profound
that I can lose myself
in you

and so find peace.[1]

In the Gospel passage for today, Jesus does not invite us to almsgiving, prayer, and fasting for their own sake. They are but responses to a God who is first asking each of us to allow God to love us. It is that love which transforms us. From within the loving embrace of that relationship we begin a journey where we seek to name our movements toward and away from God.

As we receive the exquisite mark of Love on our foreheads, we commit ourselves to enter as fully as possible into that unique relationship with God. Then, as Jesus promises, God, "who sees in secret, will reward you." The measure of effective almsgiving, prayer, and fasting will be the reward of peace.

First Sunday of Lent
Matthew 4:1-11

✤ Matthew tells us Jesus "fasted forty days and forty nights, and afterward he was famished." The word "famished" implies a great emptiness, an extreme hunger. Such emptiness brings great vulnerability. In this vulnerable state, Jesus is approached by the tempter.

The encounter begins in the desert wilderness, progresses to the pinnacle of the temple and then moves to a high mountain where Jesus can see the splendor of the world's kingdoms. At each place the tempter offers Jesus something to fill the void, and each time Jesus declines.

What the tempter fails to recognize is a paradox: As the tempter literally takes Jesus higher, Jesus moves downward more and more deeply into total identification with our human situation. His vulnerability will be the catalyst that ultimately saves humanity.

We have just begun another wilderness journey. How deeply are we willing to enter into and own our humanity? How "famished" will we dare to become? Are we willing to trust, like Jesus, the God who fills us, the God who will send angels to wait on us? Each time the stakes seem high, can we surrender to the faithful companion who embraces us as he embraces all humanity? We can, because we never do this alone.

I thought this hunger mine alone
until I saw your desert table spread
with loaves of stones you could have changed to bread.[2]

Second Sunday of Lent
Matthew 17:1–9

✣ Matthew's Gospel account of the transfiguration is preceded by two interesting encounters between Jesus and Peter. When Jesus asks his disciples, "Who do you say that I am?" it is Peter who answers, "You are the Messiah, the Son of the living God." After that, Jesus began to show his disciples what that meant: He must go to Jerusalem, undergo great suffering, be killed and on the third day be raised.

This precipitates another encounter where Peter takes Jesus aside and rebukes him, "God forbid it, Lord! This must never happen to you" (Matthew 16:15–16, 22). Peter recognizes his friend as the Messiah, the fulfillment of the traditions of the past and the embodiment of all his hopes and dreams, but he is not prepared to let that same friend carry out the mission for which he came. Peter is not yet ready to understand the depth of God's love for him and humanity.

Jesus lets Peter struggle with what seems so incongruous for a while; then "[s]ix days later Jesus took with him Peter and James and his brother John and led them up a high mountain, by themselves." There Jesus is transfigured before Peter and his other close friends.

His face shines like the sun and he talks with Moses and Elijah. Suddenly a bright cloud overshadows them: the two who represent the Law and the Prophets and the one who is their fulfillment. Perhaps at this point Peter gets some clarity about his own declaration that Jesus is the Messiah. Peter has little time to process the insight because out of the cloud a voice says, "This is my Son, the Beloved; with him I am well pleased; listen to him!" The disciples fall to the ground in fear until Jesus touches them and tells them not to be afraid. When they look up, they see only Jesus.

> Once more they ventured from the Dust to raise
> Their eyes—up to the Throne—into the Blaze,
> And in the Centre of the Glory there
> Beheld the Figure of—Themselves—as 'twere
> Transfigured—looking to Themselves, beheld
> The Figure on the Throne en-miracled,
> Until their Eyes themselves and That between
> Did hesitate which Seer was, which Seen;
> They That, That They: Another, yet the Same;
> Dividual, yet One: from whom there came
> A Voice of awful Answer, scarce discern'd,
> From which to Aspiration whose return'd
> They scarcely knew; as when some Man apart
> Answers aloud the Question in his Heart:
> "The Sun of my Perfection is a Glass
> Wherein from Seeing into Being pass."[3]

Peter, James, and John, the witnesses of Jesus' transfiguration, are themselves transfigured. As they hear the voice that tells them to listen to Jesus, they are changed. That voice claims and affirms them too as they become deeply aware of God within. Only with that awareness can they comprehend the depth of God's love that they will soon witness in Jesus' suffering, death and resurrection.

We know Peter will stumble again and again before Jesus fulfills his mission. But, Peter leaves that mountain experience of transfiguration somehow transformed as well. He has been "Seer," but his own self-understanding has been expanded; he is also "Seen."

Peter answered Jesus' question, "Who do you say that I am?" with an insight yet to be affirmed. Now that same question can be put to the transfigured/transformed Peter himself, "Who do you say that you are?" And Peter answers aloud the question in his heart:

> "The Sun of my Perfection is a Glass
> Wherein from Seeing into Being pass."

Third Sunday of Lent
John 4:5-42

✤ Today's Gospel passage is a tender love story that is best understood if one begins at the end. When the crucified Jesus "knew that
it was all now finished, he said (in order to fulfill the Scripture),
"I am thirsty" (John 19:28). Jesus' words, spoken from his human
need, are also uttered from his divinity.

God's eternal yearning for us, for our faith and love, is at the
core of our deepest longing. The story of Jesus' encounter with the
woman at the well is a metaphor for the thirst that is fundamental to
our relationship with God. We know that our hearts beat in concert
with God's heart when we say in unison, "We thirst."

Thirst led the woman to the well. Hers was an action that had
become almost mindless except for the lonely ache in her heart which
no amount of water could quench. Cut off from the social support
of the other women who journeyed together to the well, her trips
to gather water alone left her feeling more parched. But one day a
man met her at that place of deep thirst and said, "Give me a drink."

Jesus' request seems simple even though it broke all of the social
and religious norms of the day. The conversation that follows takes
the woman deeper into her own heart where she can finally name
the insatiable desire that only a God who also thirsts can fulfill.
This is no chance encounter.

Jesus could have taken another route but he chose not to bypass
the Samaritans, whom his Jewish compatriots avoided, as they held
them in disdain. God could take another route, perhaps a more regal
way, to engage with humanity. But God chose to be embodied in
One who would cry, "I am thirsty....Give me a drink."

This mutual thirst changed the Samaritan woman's life. Her
encounter with Jesus became in her "a spring of water gushing up
to eternal life." Perhaps she returned many times to the well by
herself. Now she came alone not because of social constraints but
because this well was the place where she finally met someone who
understood her thirst. This is where she prayed.

With my Beloved I alone have been.
When secrets tenderer than evening airs
Passed, and the Vision blest
Was granted to my prayers.
That crowned me, else obscure, with endless fame;
The while amazed between
His Beauty and His Majesty
I stood in silent ecstasy
Revealing that which o'er my spirit went and came.
Lo, in His face commingled
Is every charm and grace;
The whole of Beauty singled
Into a perfect face
Beholding Him would cry,
'There is no God but He, and He is the most High.'[4]

How her prayer must slake God's thirst!

Fourth Sunday of Lent
John 9:1–41

✤ One day I was driving behind a cargo van that had the words "Caution: Blind Man Driving" emblazoned on the back doors. The van belonged to a company that sold window blinds, but their words of caution caused people to do a kind of double take.

Today's Gospel passage invites us to look again as well. There is more than meets the eye (pardon the pun) than Jesus curing a man who had been blind from birth. The man's physical blindness is simply an entree´ for Jesus to challenge his followers, the onlookers, and the religious and civil authorities to examine their own blindness.

The first group that Jesus challenges is his own disciples. Upon seeing the man on the side of the road as they walked with Jesus, the disciples begin speculating about whose sin caused the man's blindness: the man's or his parents'.

The disciples don't see the man or make any attempt to serve him in any way. They are simply people of their times who never questioned the commonly held belief that illness was the result of sin. Jesus quickly shifts his disciples from their academic exercise to the work of healing the man, using the very ground beneath their feet and his own saliva to make a mud pack. Can the disciples see that Jesus prefers action on behalf of another over theory?

Then the man's neighbors get into the act. They don't really see the man himself. He has become a common fixture along their daily paths. So when he returns from the pool of Siloam healed, they begin to talk among themselves about whether it is the same man. How indifferent must the townspeople have been if they can't tell that this is the same person?

The cure has caused such a flurry of theorizing among the man's neighbors that they take him to the religious authorities, the Pharisees. The Pharisees focus on Jesus' failure to observe the Sabbath. They can't see beyond the age-old Law and the Prophets to the one who fulfills both. Are they so entrenched in their assumptions that they can't even see the facts?

The Jews simply refuse to believe that the man was blind from the start. They quiz his parents, who affirm that the man was blind from birth but they shy away from the speculation around how he was cured.

Out of fear, they pass the responsibility for answering on to their now-seeing son. The son's answers so challenge the Jews that they drive him out. What keeps the Jews from accepting the truth about the healing of the man and the man who is the healer?

The lesson Jesus wants the other players in the story to learn is that spiritual blindness is the real sin. We all know that. The challenge comes when we summon the courage to ask where our own blind spots might be.

We are the disciples, the neighbors, the Pharisees, and the Jews. The questions that apply to each group apply also to us. Perhaps the insights of Meister Eckhart will both challenge and encourage us to seek a cure for our own blindness.

A man
    born blind can easily ·
    deny the magnificence of a vast landscape.

  He can easily deny all the wonders that he cannot touch,
    smell, taste, or hear.

    But one day the wind will show you its kindness
      and remove the tiny patches that
      covered our eyes,

    and we will see God more clearly
        than we have ever seen
        ourselves.[5]

Fifth Sunday of Lent
John 11:1–45

✤ In the meantime…. Many stories are so complex with different
yet related twists and turns that take place simultaneously that it's
impossible to tell them without using phrases like "in the meantime."
Today's Gospel is just such a story.

   We enter the story at the point where Jesus' dear friend Lazarus
is gravely ill with some unnamed disease, and his sisters Martha
and Mary send word to Jesus expecting that he will drop everything
and rush to Lazarus' side. Jesus hears about Lazarus but stays where
he is two more days. When he does decide to go back to Judea his
disciples remind him that the last time he was there the Jews tried
to stone him. He finally tells them that Lazarus is dead.

   In the meantime, back in Bethany the bereaved Martha and Mary
are being consoled by their neighbors. When word gets to them that
Jesus is finally on his way Martha goes out to meet him on the road.
Mary stays at home. When Martha meets Jesus she greets him with
the comment that if he had been there, Lazarus would not have died.

   What follows is an interesting theological conversation about
death and resurrection. Then the sisters reverse roles—Mary goes out

to talk to Jesus and Martha stays home. The conversation between Mary and Jesus echoes the previous conversation.

The staging of this drama with multiple settings would prove to be quite challenging, so it is good that the three lead characters— Jesus, Martha, and Mary—finally gather at one place, the tomb of Lazarus. However, while the setting is simple, the conversation between Jesus and Martha seems to hover in different planes. At last, the stone is removed and the "dead" Lazarus comes out of the cave trailing the burial wrappings.

This string of parallel events might be a metaphor for our own struggle to understand death and resurrection. We profess faith in the resurrection yet can be apprehensive about that promise when physical death is imminent.

Today we might try to let the drama play out in our hearts through the emotions of Jesus, Martha, and Mary. Perhaps we will learn to accept the inevitability of suffering and death and strengthen our trust and faith in the resurrection as we let Jesus' promise take root at ever deeper levels of our being.

We might even invite Lazarus to offer his insights:

After one moment when I bowed my head
And the whole world turned over and came upright,
And I came out where the old road shone white,
I walked the ways and heard what all men said,
Forests of tongues, like autumn leaves unshed,
Being not unlovable but strange and light;
Old riddles and new creeds, not in despite
But softly, as men smile about the dead.

The sages have a hundred maps to give
That trace their crawling cosmos like a tree.
They rattle reason out through many a sieve
That stores the sand and lets the gold go free:
And all these things are less than dust to me
Because my name is Lazarus and I live.[6]

Palm Sunday of the Lord's Passion
Matthew 26:14—27:66

✤ Today's liturgy invites us into a challenging mix of palms carried in triumphant procession as well as a parade of human betrayals. Our own hearts move in figurative procession from shouts of hosanna to shouts of condemnation. As we begin this week we call holy, each of us needs to take measure of our hearts. The Venerable Bede might be the barometer we need for this task.

> Blind with old age, the Venerable Bede
> Ceased not, for that, to preach and publish forth
> The news from heaven,—the tidings of great joy.
> From town to town—through all the villages—
> With trusty guidance, roamed the aged saint,
> And preached the word with all the fire of youth.
>
> One day his boy had led him to a vale
> That lay all thickly sowed with mighty rocks.
> In mischief more than malice spake the boy:
> "Most reverend father! there are many men
> Assembled here, who wait to hear thy voice."
>
> The blind old man, so bowed, straightway rose up,
> Chose him his text, expounded, then applied,
> Exhorted, warned, rebuked, and comforted,
> So fervently, that soon the gushing tears
> Streamed thick and fast down to his hoary beard.
> When, at the close, as seemeth always meet,
> He prayed, "Our Father," and pronounced aloud,
> "Thine is the kingdom and the power,—thine
> The glory now and through eternity,"—
> At once there rang through all that echoing vale
> A sound of many thousand voices crying,
> "Amen! most reverend sire, amen! amen!"

Trembling with terror and remorse, the boy
Knelt down before the saint, and owned his sin.
"Son," said the old man, "hast thou then never read,
'When men are dumb, the stones shall cry aloud'?—
Henceforward mock not, son, the word of God!
Living it is, and mighty, cutting sharp,
Like a two-edged sword. And when the heart
Of flesh grows hard and stubborn as the stone,
A heart of flesh shall stir in stones themselves!"[7]

The poet tells us that "the Word of God!/Living it is, and mighty, cutting sharp." Our task as we process into Holy Week is to measure how well we recognize God's Word today as living. The Gospel falls on us as on stones if we fail to recognize the ways the passion continues to be enacted in our midst. Yet we trust that "a heart of flesh shall stir in stones themselves!"

Holy Thursday
1 Corinthians 11:23–26; John 13:1–15

✚ It is interesting that on this day when we commemorate the institution of the Eucharist, our Gospel passage is from John and, unlike the other three Gospel writers, John does not include an account of the institution of the Eucharist.

Instead, this evening as we gather to celebrate the Eucharist we hear the account of the institution of the Eucharist from Paul while John focuses on Jesus washing the feet of his disciples. Perhaps this is an invitation to us to reflect on how we integrate what we celebrate around the altar with how we interact with others when we "go in peace to love and serve the Lord."

In a very real sense, John implies Jesus' total giving of himself in the Eucharist as he situates the Passover celebration in the larger context of Jesus very mission: "Having loved his own who were in the world, he loved them to the end."

The washing of the disciples' feet is not an isolated act but one that springs from a love that has known the reality of great suffering. From his birth, Jesus' family knew displacement. Rejection and hunger haunted him as he read it in the eyes and hearts of those he encountered in the temple and in the countryside.

He knew the human condition which he had humbly embraced. Washing the feet of those he loved is an expression of his understanding of the mission that had been entrusted to him.

After this tender action, Jesus commissions his followers to do the same: "So if I, your Lord and Teacher, have washed your feet, you also ought to wash one another's feet. For I have set you an example, that you also should do as I have done to you."

These words are challenging and can only be fully embraced when we hear the echo of "this is my body which will be given up for you. This is the cup of my blood, the blood of the new and everlasting covenant. It will be shed for you and for all so that sins may be forgiven. Do this in memory of me."

So, on this Holy Thursday, we are handed a precious "Legacy."

> When he was a child
> his mother told him
> of how she and Joseph
> had been turned away
> from their ancestral home—
> the House of Bread—
> on the night of his birth.
>
> The story taught him
> that rejection and hunger
> gnawed with the same teeth.
>
> Grown, he walked through
> towns and countryside,
> feeding hollow-eyed hundreds
> who pursued him by day.

But a bottomless ocean
of hungry mouths
flooded his dreams.

He learned that the memory
of yesterday's bread
could not relieve today's hunger.

On the eve of his death
he at last found a way
to keep rejection and hunger
at bay. He held his life in his hands
and said to his friends,
"Take. Eat. This is my body,
broken for you."

And when they were filled, commanded:
"Feed the hungry. Do this.
Remember me."[8]

Do we have the courage to say, "Amen!" and
"Thanks be to God!"

GOOD FRIDAY
The Passion of Our Lord Jesus Christ
John Chapters 18–19

✤ It is not unusual for the motion picture industry to provide audiences with one or more movie sequels. Whether or not it was in the minds of the writers, producers, and directors at the time of the making of the first movie, somehow the plot doesn't seem finished—there's more life in the main characters, and the story line has more twists and turns to unfold.

It even happens that sometimes, when all the sequels seem to have exhausted the story, a prequel is issued and we learn what happened to the characters before the first movie drew us into its intrigues.

Today we are invited to reflect with John on what happens to Jesus in the sequence of one day: from the time after he eats the Passover meal with his friends until the next evening when he is laid in the tomb. The first scene takes place in a garden across the Kidron valley.

The final scene in today's drama is also set in a garden where Jesus is placed in a tomb adjacent to where he was crucified. As we listen to the account, our minds can easily write the prequel as well as a sequel. We know the entire story of Jesus' life, death, and resurrection well. The story doesn't change, so neither the book by Fulton Oursler nor the movie of *The Greatest Story Ever Told* have a prequel or sequel.

Yet, each Good Friday we gather with the faith community as at a wake to retell the story and let the memories of how we have each been personally and profoundly touched by this man Jesus play over and over in our hearts.

It happens every year: we gather to pray together because we need to draw strength from each other. Each time we hear the story we become more aware of the contrasts between his story and our story. Our sobs may be as much about our failures as about the death of the Lord. Patrick F. Kirby's "Sequel to Finality" provides a kind of examination of conscience:

They drove the hammered nails into His hands,
His hands that shaped the hot sun overhead;
Then all prepared to return to their own lands,
Glad in the knowledge God at last was dead.

"Now Babel can be built, and none deny!
In its cool gardens shall we take our ease;
Nor need we fear the everseeing eye,—
Our gods shall be whatever gods we please.

"Ishtar shall guard us, mother of all men,
And Bel rejoice us when the winds blow spiced
From Indus. Wine and song shall glad us then,—
We never loved this wistful, pallid Christ!"

Even as we review our personal and communal journeys that began weeks ago with a brush of ashes and the intent to "turn from sin and be faithful to the gospel" and own the times we detoured from the paths to which we had committed ourselves; we also know that this has been a time of grace and we have allowed God to settle more deeply into our hearts.

We leave the Good Friday service to spend the next day in quiet journey through a garden. As we leave the faith community, it is important to reflect on the final two lines of Kirby's poem:

So each rode homeward. And by each one's side
Unseen One rode, Who had been crucified.[9]

Today God invites each of us to write a sequel to *The Greatest Story Ever Told* because God will never call it finished until our hearts beat in rhythm with God's heart and we sing with full voice a never-ending Alleluia.

NOTES

1. Vanek, Elizabeth-Anne, "The Wounding," in *Woman Dreamer*, (Bristol, Indiana: Windham Hall Press, 1989), 32.
2. Zimmerman, Irene, "Companion," in *Incarnation*, (Cambridge: Cowley Publications, 2004), 140.
3. Attar, "The Birds Find Their King," trans. by Edward Fitzgerald in *Poetry for the Spirit*, (London: Watkins Publishing, 2002), 58.
4. Rabi'a, "With My Beloved Alone," in *Poetry for the Spirit*, (London: Watkins Publishing, 2002), 44.
5. Eckhart, Meister, "The Wind Will Show Its Kindness," trans. by Daniel Ladinsky in *Love Poems from God*, (New York: Penguin Compass, 2002), 93.
6. Chesterton, G. K., "The Convert," in *The Golden Book of Catholic Poetry*, edited by Alfred Noyes, (Philadelphia: J. B. Lippincott Company, 1946), 262.
7. Kosegarten, Ludwig Theobul, "The Amen of the Stones," in *Divine Inspiration: The Life of Jesus in World Poetry* edited by Robert Atwan, George Dardess and Peggy Rosenthal, (New York" Oxford University Press, 1998), 334-5.
8. Zimmerman, Irene, "Legacy," in *Incarnation*, (Cambridge: Cowley Publications, 2004), 92-3.
9. Kirby, Patrick F., "Sequel to Finality," in *The Golden Book of Catholic Poetry*, edited by Alfred Noyes, (Philadelphia: J. B. Lippincott Company, 1946), 317.

Easter

EASTER SUNDAY
Resurrection of the Lord
Matthew 28:1–10

✣ "As the first day of the week was dawning…." It's Easter Sunday morning and we get up in a kind of haze. While we are still awash in the glow of the new fire kindled among us and in our hearts when we gathered in vigil last night, there is also a sense of unbelief. It takes good news a while to seep into our consciousness.

Last night we held candles, listened to the wonderful story of God's journey with us and proclaimed our belief in the God who lived as one of us, died, and rose to new life. It does make our heads spin.

Matthew's Easter account seems to capture our thoughts at dawn. As we join Mary Magdalene and the other Mary as they go to the tomb, we trip along suspended between grief and an inexplicable sense of hope. The Gospel writer does not share with us any doubts on the part of the two women as the angel tells them that Jesus has been raised.

We probably don't overtly express any doubts either. Yet, our Easter joy is undergirded by the griefs and anxieties that mark us as human. Like Mary Magdalene and the other Mary, we leave the tomb "with fear and great joy."

Then Jesus himself enters the scene. "Greetings! Do not be afraid…." Can we suspend our fears and all those doubts that stand in the way of total trust in this God of life? The women in this Gospel passage "came to him, took hold of his feet, and worshiped him." If we reflect once more on the story, perhaps we, too, can take hold of his feet:

> The heady fragrances they carried
> rose above their heads like incense,
> exorcising the garden of death.
> "Who will roll way the stone for us?"
> the women whispered to one another.

> Earlier, in the near-dawn darkness,
> they had posed the question to the others—
> as request, not challenge.
> They had no heart to challenge the flock
> hiding in terror behind secret doors.

> None of the men had offered to go,
> so the women had set out in haste alone
> to straighten twisted feet and fingers,
> comb black blood from matted hair,
> anoint the precious body with spices.

> "But who _will_ roll away the stone?"
> They whispered again as they neared the tomb.
> "Jesus said prayer could move mountains.
> We must stay together, continue to believe."
> They stepped firmly forward, balancing their heavy jars.

> When they looked up, they saw that the stone,
> which was very large, had already been rolled back.
> Inside, they heard from a being dressed in light:
> "You are looking for Jesus who was crucified.
> He has been raised; he is not here."

Fleeing from the tomb,
intent on telling no one,
they tripped pell-mell over terror and amazement
onto the glowing feet of Jesus.
"Go, tell the others!" he commanded.

After the telling, they set out in haste—
together this time, a community of equals—
to roll away stones, straighten crooked paths,
comb the far countries,
anoint the precious world with Good News.[1]

Perhaps now we can let go of the doubts that nag us and embrace the new possibilities that resurrection opens up for us. Jesus doesn't just tell us, "Do not be afraid." He adds, "[G]o and tell my brothers [and sisters] to go to Galilee; there they will see me." Then, as a community of equals, we will be able to make good on our baptismal promises. We will set out in haste "to roll away stones, straighten crooked paths,/comb the far countries,/anoint the precious world with Good News."

Second Sunday of Easter
John 20:19–31

✢ How do people recognize the signs of Jesus within our faith community? Perhaps it is not in perfectly sung hymns but in the fact that we want to sing together regardless of how well we sing. Maybe it's not in well-run meetings but in people planning and actually working together to accomplish some good for others.

It might not be in how we greet the nicely dressed person who sits in front of us but in how we meet the homeless person who slips into the row behind us. While good choirs, well-planned agendas and personal hygiene are important, they are not necessarily the measure of a person or a group.

When Jesus appears to his disciples fearfully locked in the house, he doesn't sport a shiny halo. Rather, he shows them his scarred hands and his side. And, as if that wasn't proof enough, he came back the next week and asked Thomas to actually touch those scars.

Today we pray, perhaps because of and certainly in spite of, the scars of sorrow and hurt that mark our own lives. We bring them as well as the joy of Easter faith to share with the faith community.

How we deal with our personal and communal "scars" may be a measure of how much we are able to recognize and even touch the risen Jesus who appears among us. Consider that Jesus, who had cured so many people, chose to bear the scars of his death in his resurrected body.

> When Christ came from the shadows by the stream
> By Phlegethon,
> Scars were upon his feet, his hands, his side.
>   Not, as dulled souls might deem,
>   That He, who had the power
> Of healing all the wounds whereof men died,
>   Could not have healed his own,
> But that those scars had some divinity,
>   Carriage of mystery,
> Life's source to bear the stigmata of Death.
>
> By these same scars his men
> Behind the very body that they knew,
>   Not transient breath,
>   No drift of bodiless air,
> And held him in their hearts in fortress there.
> They knew their Master risen, and unfurled
> The hope of resurrection through the world.
>
> By these same scars, in prayer for all mankind,
>   Before his Father's face,
> He pleads our wounds within his mortal flesh,
> And all the travail of his mortal days:

For ever interceding for His grace,
Remembering where forgetfulness were blind,
For ever pitiful, for ever kind,
Instant that Godhead should take thought for man,
Remembering the manhood of His Son,
His only Son, and the deep wounds he bore.

By these same scars his folk will not give o'er
Office of worship, whilst they see,
Passion, thy mystery:
In those dark wounds their weal,
In that descent to hell their climb to the stars,
His death, their life,
Their wreath, his crown of thorns.[2]

Our Easter faith doesn't take away the wounds; rather, it transforms them.

Third Sunday of Easter
Luke 24:13-35

✠ Like their Jewish ancestors whose journey with God kept taking them farther and farther from their comfortable origins, the disciples who are making the seven-mile trek from Jerusalem to Emmaus are on a journey that seems to be on the fold of their map—fuzzy and requiring some mental and physical gymnastics to read.

For God's Chosen People, each time they thought they found a solution to one set of problems—slavery, floods, exile—God seemed to give them a new set of hard-to-read maps, new goals. So, for the disciples en route to Emmaus, the one whom they thought would be the one to redeem Israel had died.

The route seemed circuitous. Sure, the women had gone to the tomb and got the word from angels that Jesus was alive, but where was he now?

As Jesus joins these disillusioned companions on their journey, he tries to help them move beyond Israel's faith in the future of the nation to faith in him and the mystery of his death and resurrection.

He invites them to see the thread connecting the events they just experienced in Jerusalem with the events related in the Hebrew Scriptures. "Then beginning with Moses and all the prophets, he interpreted to them the things about himself in all the Scriptures." Yet he is still a stranger to them. The map of their experience doesn't allow for such convergence.

We also can rely too much on maps, on pre-planned itineraries that don't allow for the wonders on unexpected paths. The person walking alongside Cleopas and his companion is perhaps too close for them to recognize.

Yet something must have been stirring in them as they invite him to stay with them. That evening, "When he was at table with them, he took bread, blessed and broke it, and gave it to them. Then their eyes were opened, and they recognized him; and he vanished from their sight."

The paradox is that Jesus was more present to them on their journey, even in their despair and doubt, than when they actually recognized him and finally believed. In retrospect they say to each other, "Were not our hearts burning within us while he was talking to us on the road, while he was opening the Scriptures to us?"

Denise Levertov gives us an opportunity to reflect on this paradox of closeness and distance in her poem, "The Servant-Girl at Emmaus," which is about a painting by that name done by Velázquez.

She listens, listens, holding
her breath. Surely that voice
is his—the one
who had looked at her, once, across the crowd,
as no one ever had looked?
Had seen her? Has spoken as if to her?

Surely those hands were his,
taking the platter of bread from hers just now?

Hands he'd laid on the dying and made them well?

Surely that face—?

The man they'd crucified for sedition and blasphemy.
The man whose body disappeared from its tomb.
The man it was rumored now some women had seen this
 morning, alive?

Those who had brought this stranger home to their table
don't recognize yet with whom they sit.
But she in the kitchen, absently touching
 the wine jug she's to take in,
a young Black servant intently listening,

swings round and sees
the light around him
and is sure.[3]

God journeys alongside each of us even when, especially when, we least expect it; and that makes every road the road to Emmaus. This is not a time for maps. Rather, it is a time for "absently touching/the wine jug" and like the Servant Girl, "intently listening."

Fourth Sunday of Easter

John 10:1–10

✜ Sometimes it's hard for us to comprehend the intimacy that God desires with each of us. It is not enough that God became a human being and lived among us; we seem to need frequent reminders of God's presence within and around us.

Jesus uses the image of a shepherd and sheep to help his followers grasp such intimacy. His Middle Eastern followers in particular would resonate with the meaning of such imagery.

Sheep herding practices in Jesus' time often included the use of circular walls of stones covered with briars to house the sheep overnight. A small opening was left for the sheep to pass in and out of the enclosure. There was not a gate as our experience would suggest.

Rather, the shepherd was the gate. After all of the sheep were inside, the shepherd would lie across the opening so that nothing could get in or out of the sheepfold without first encountering the shepherd.

Jesus, whom we call the Good Shepherd, tells us, "Very truly, I tell you, I am the gate for the sheep." And, in the verse following today's Gospel passage he says, "I am the good shepherd. The good shepherd lays down his life for the sheep." Jesus completes the circle of God's embrace and gives his very life in the process.

Felix Lope de Vega Y Carpio gives voice to our hearts in his sonnet:

> Shepherd who with your tender calls
> From deep slumber has wakened me,
> You who made this log the staff
> On which your powerful arms are held,
>
> Upon my faith turn your pitying eyes,
> For I confess you my love and lord,
> And to follow you pledge my word,
> Your beauteous feet and calls so mild.
>
> Hear me, Shepherd who dies for love,
> Flinch not at my frightful sins,
> You to the humbled so much a friend
> Stay, and let my cares be heard...
> Though why do I ask that you stay for me,
> When to make you stay your feet are nailed?[4]

It is not God who wanders away from relationships. We are the ones who stray. But Jesus calls us to be people of hope in spite of our sin. *"You to the humbled so much a friend,/...When to make you stay your feet are nailed."*

The poet reminds us of Peter's promise, "...by his wounds you have been healed. For you were going astray like sheep, but now you have returned to the shepherd and guardian of your souls." (I Peter 2:24-5) We know Peter's journey in and out of intimacy with God, so to have such assurance from him gives us the courage to listen more intently for the voice of the One who keeps calling us back.

It may take a lifetime to fully understand that God really desires an intimate relationship with each of us. Meantime we grasp for images that remind us: "I came that they may have life, and have it abundantly."

Fifth Sunday of Easter
John 14:1-12

✤ Today few people would set out on a long journey to new places without the benefit of maps, guidebooks, and satellite-powered directional systems. Before leaving home, most travelers have a potential route and reserved lodging as well as particular places that they believe will hopefully be highlights to be remembered with pictures and postcards.

So, most of us can understand that, as Jesus prepares the disciples for his own departure, they want some of the same assurances. The one who has been their guide is going away to prepare a place for them, and it doesn't appear that he is leaving a map.

A few short years before the disciples had dropped everything to follow this itinerant preacher. All they had were dreams of a Messiah. Their leader seemed to follow no visible map or guidebook and they had quickly learned that lodging would always be questionable. Yet, one would suppose that the disciples reached a point where they became somewhat comfortable with Jesus' unwritten agenda and actually discovered a certain freedom in trusting his sense of direction.

But, as we hear in today's Gospel passage, Jesus is inviting them to a new and potentially scary place and they lose that sense of trust. He tells them, "Do not let your hearts be troubled. Believe in God, believe also in me." Yet they are full of questions: "Lord, we do not know where you are going. How can we know the way?" "Lord, show us the Father and we will be satisfied."

We are all on that same unmapped journey and know that same uncertainty. The Jesus who speaks to his followers in today's Gospel passage believes they are ready for the next milepost on their journey.

He wants to make sure they know their internal compasses are true and can be trusted. They balk at this, just as we do. Who can trust that the journey inward has been sufficient to support the next steps? Where is the assurance that we <u>do</u> know the way?

Jesus' first-century disciples figured it out and, as the Acts of the Apostles attest, they were able to do even "greater works." Most of us still have to plumb the depths and find that sense of trust in God—and in ourselves.

Fortunately, we are blessed with people among us who seem so certain and we wonder how they got to that place. We suspect that neither they nor Jesus' disciples before them came to that place easily. There is comfort in that.

Perhaps we will have to leave behind our own maps. Maybe the highlights of the journey will not be found in photographs but will be carried in our hearts. And, most importantly, we could find that we are no longer in the driver's seat.

> In the convent of Perpetual Adoration
> on an eternal summer afternoon
> the three o'clock chimes called back
> the flight of the old nun.
> In her wheelchair
> before the God who lives in bread
> and runs the risk of staleness
> she watched the hour
> that Peter, James and John did not.

Two young ones come for her
with the precise steps of piety
and perpendicular genuflections.
The guard is changed.
She is pushed from the adoration space
but the bright white God goes with her
in the monstrance behind her dimming eyes.
The sacred has performed its slow alchemy.
The wheelchair hypnotically clacks
the revolutions of her exit.
She is maneuvered by the sister on duty
to a sparse clean room with a crucifix and flowers
and placed in the windowed light
where she dwells with silence
and the memory of praise and
the dancing particles of the undying sun.[5]

Sometimes we find our journey marked quite comfortably
"with the precise steps of piety/and perpendicular genuflections."
At other times we are quite happily helping others get "placed in the
windowed light." Discipleship is, after all, about prayer and action
on behalf of others.

But, in spite of this, we all long for the time when we know without
doubt that "the bright white God goes with [us]/in the monstrance
behind [our] dimming eyes" and we can dwell "…with silence/and
the memory of praise." Then we will know with certainty that Jesus
is "the way, and the truth, and the life."

Sixth Sunday of Easter
John 14:15–21

✤ Ben Franklin is credited with saying, "In this world nothing can be said to be certain, except death and taxes." Franklin's statement carries humor as much as it conveys truth. The truth is not so much about the inevitability of death and taxes as much as it is the fact that this world is characterized by vagaries. Who and what can you really count on?

The passage from John's Gospel today invites us to step beyond the realm of worldly certainty and reflect on the one of whom Jesus says, "You know him, because he abides with you, and he will be in you." Jesus is talking about "the Spirit of Truth, whom the world cannot receive, because it neither sees him nor knows him." So, we live in a world of death and taxes. How do we recognize the Spirit of Truth?

Jesus uses an interesting title for the Spirit, one which he applies to himself as well: "I will ask the Father, and he will give you another Advocate, to be with you forever."

An advocate is one who pleads for, argues for, supports, defends, protects, advances the rights of another. It's a strong role and one that Jesus wants to assure us is his way and the Spirit's way of accompanying us. We are the ones who forget that certainty, so today Jesus reminds us:

I am with you when you're running out of wine
at your child's wedding feast
and you know the shame of it will last forever.
I will be for you the Best Wine of all.

I am with you in your storm-tossed boat
when joy, hope, life seem lost at sea
and you come close to falling overboard.
I will still the storm, restore you to tranquility.

I am with you when you're caught out on a limb—
a social climbing tax collector, treed!
I too will climb a tree and be mocked on it.
I will honor you by coming to your house to eat.

I am with you when your body is so bent
that friendly faces, trees, sky are lost to view
and all you see are feet hurrying by.
I will empower you to stand up straight again.

I am with you when men catch you in adultery
and your death is but a stone's throw away.
I am the Gate to the sheepfold. I will lay
my body down between your enemies and you.

I am with you when you claim you do not know me.
I have prayed that you may overcome despair
and bring the heavy burden of your sin to me.
I have forgiven you ahead of time.

I am with you when your dearest friend and brother
passes through the dark door of death,
leaving you disconsolate. I know the pain of loss.
I AM the Resurrection and the Life.[6]

The poet's words touch something deep inside each one of us. We have all known what it is to feel orphaned. But more importantly, in spite of those times—perhaps because of those times—we know what it means to have an Advocate.

Today we celebrate that certainty. Ben Franklin may be correct about the fact that there is nothing certain in this world but death and taxes. Yet we live with our hearts focused on a different world, and we have experienced its promise: "In a little while the world will no longer see me, but you will see me; because I live, you also will live."

Seventh Sunday of Easter
John 17:1-11

✤ How often have you signed off on a letter with the words, "Love and Prayers?" When you hear of someone's illness or a request for prayers for a loved one, don't you let the person know that he, she, or the loved one is in your prayers?

Sometimes the only words we have to comfort someone are very brief, "I'll pray for you." Consider how many people send prayer requests to shrines and houses of prayer. We are a people who value prayer for ourselves and for others. Today's Gospel passage, then, should contain something each of us can relate to in a personal as well as a communal way.

John inserts Jesus' final prayer for his disciples in the context of his farewell discourse. The essence of his message is in the prayer itself. While the Gospels record many times when Jesus went off by himself for intimate prayer with his Father, this prayer to the Father is intended to be heard and reflected upon by his disciples of every age.

As he prays, Jesus is reporting on his commission: to glorify God on earth, to make God's name known, to enable his followers to know God, to receive and keep God's word, and to help his followers to be one.

Everything comes together in that final commission, "that they may be one, as we are one." Ultimately what Jesus has invited his followers to is a life in relationship.

That relationship with God and among Jesus' followers is to be like the relationship between Jesus and his Father. In praying about his own commission Jesus is also commissioning his disciples. Jesus is inviting his followers to be good news themselves by being a community of love.

Today, as we listen to Jesus' prayer we need to reflect on our own commission to be one, to be a community characterized by our love for each other. Consider "Christ's Message."

Christ has no hands but our hands
To do His work today;
He has no feet but our feet
To lead men in His way.

He has no tongue but our tongues
To tell men how He died;
He has no help but our help
To lead men to His side.

We are the Lord's only message
The careless world will read;
We are the sinner's Gospel,
We are the scoffer's creed.

We are the Lord's last message,
Written in deed and word.
What if the type be crooked?
What if the print be blurred?[7]

As Jesus prays in John's farewell discourse, he has deeds to back his words. In commissioning us as he prays for us, he expects the same from us. It is important that we continue to demonstrate our love for others through our prayer.

Sometimes that is all that we can offer, and it is never a small token. But we also carry a commission to be Christ's message by our deeds. So today, "Pray for me, as I will for thee, that we may merrily meet in heaven." (Thomas More) In the meantime, there's lots of crooked type and blurred print for us to attend to as well.

Ascension
Matthew 28:16–20

✤ Jesus' final words in Matthew's Gospel are, "And remember, I am with you always, to the end of the age." Unlike the accounts recorded by Mark and Luke, Matthew makes no mention of Jesus ascending. We simply understand that he left the eleven disciples at that point.

The human limitations of linear time and space have him ascend because, of course, that's where God lives. Then the practical application of Jesus' command to "go therefore and make disciples of all nations" takes precedence and we get on with the mission. Sometimes we even forget what we were told to remember: "I am with you always."

What would happen if we celebrated the Feast of the Ascension not simply as a commemoration of Jesus' return to his Father but of his promise to be with us always? What if we could escape the limitations of time and celebrate God's presence in the NOW?

There is a Celtic saying that heaven and earth are only three feet apart but in the "thin places" that distance is even smaller. What if the ascension is a "thin place"—a hallowed space and time when heaven and earth are, for a moment, one? Then the promise of Jesus, "I am with you always, to the end of the age" would echo in our hearts and what joy we would experience.

If we were among the eleven disciples coming down from the mountain in Galilee, we would know a readiness for life in the world without the physical presence of Jesus because we would know that God is in the air we breathe, in our best thoughts and in the good deeds we perform.

That would make ascension happen every day because each day we would experience Jesus ascending to new glory everywhere in our lives. We would pray each day to recognize the magnificence and wonder of God's presence and want to be witnesses of God's glory among all the nations.

The disciples' readiness for life, and ours as well, is expressed beautifully in John Gillespie Magee Jr.'s poem "High Flight."

Oh! I have slipped the surly bonds of Earth
And danced the skies on laughter-silvered wings;
Sunward I've climbed, and joined the tumbling mirth
Of sun-split clouds—and done a hundred things
You have not dreamed of—wheeled and soared and swung
High in the sunlit silence. Hov'ring there,
I've chased the shouting wind along, and flung
My eager craft through footless halls of air…
Up, up the long, delirious, burning blue
I've topped the wind-swept heights with easy grace.
Where never lark, or even eagle, flew;
And, while with silent, lifting mind I've trod
The high untrespassed sanctity of space,
Put out my hand, and touched the face of God.[8]

Many of the images the poet uses are borrowed from other aviators just as lines from his poem have been used on headstones and quoted in books, movies and on TV shows. President Ronald Reagan quoted from "High Flight" in his speech following the Challenger disaster in 1986.

Magee wrote the poem just a few months before his own death at age nineteen when his aircraft was involved in a mid-air collision. He enclosed the poem on the back of a letter to his parents.

There are obvious parallels to draw but perhaps the most important thing is that we all depend on each other to remind us of Jesus' promise, "I am with you always, to the end of the age." Were the disciples "heady" with God's presence? Are we "heady" with God's presence on this feast of the Ascension? Perhaps optimists touch into the "thin places" that Magee suggests more often than others, but all of us have at some points in our life felt that "sanctity of space."

Today offers us an opportunity to remind each other of that sacred promise that Jesus left with us. Let's celebrate as our prayer helps us to slip "the surly bonds of Earth" and join "the tumbling mirth" of Son-split clouds. Rejoice!

Pentecost
John 20:19-23

✤ Anyone who has ever served on a board, a task force or any kind of a committee knows how tedious meetings can be. Yet, the intent of such gatherings is to optimize the gifts of each person for the common good.

When this doesn't happen, people become discouraged, even cynical, and their individual and collective gifts are lost to the larger community. When we truly learn to share our gifts, the tedium is diminished because there is a kind of synergy that extends beyond the group.

It's good for each of us who is part of a faith community, whether we serve on a committee or not, to remember that Pentecost happened at a gathering of people, a kind of meeting—albeit there was no agenda other than the shared fear of a community which had just been through an unbelievable experience.

They had lost their leader and were gathered presumably in prayer as well as in support of each other. Each person gathered in the meeting room had experienced God's presence in unique and intimate ways, particularly in relation to Jesus, their fallen leader. But this was not the time to wait in solitude. They waited for their God to comfort and assure them in the midst of their friends. Subconsciously at least, they wanted God to do something for their faith community.

Then Jesus appears in their midst with scarred hands and side and saying not once but twice, "Peace be with you." What comfort each must have felt! It is in the midst of their shared comfort in seeing Jesus again that Jesus says, "Receive the Holy Spirit. If you forgive the sins of any, they are forgiven them; if you retain the sins of any, they are retained."

Each person receives the Spirit and at the same time they collectively are charged with the forgiveness of each other's sins. Forgiveness adds another dimension to the gift of the Spirit. It's like Jesus knew that even though each person had the gift of the Spirit, no one person could serve all the needs of the community alone.

There would be times when each person would fail to recognize and use the gifts that the Spirit had given for the common good. There would also be times when they would fail to recognize each other's gifts. They might even be jealous of those gifts that others seemed to have in such abundance.

Today's feast of Pentecost is a celebration of the birth of the Christian community which we call Church. This faith community, like any committee, is only as strong as the commitment of each member. So today we start with ourselves.

> Lord, I did not choose to be comforted.
> I am not ready to bear the many things
> you have yet to say: you said it yourself.
> But you have sent me (against my will) your comforter
> and what is comfort but an iron command?
>
> I don't want to obey. I won't. Yes: I will.
> Why must I interrupt my self-indulgent weakness
> to respond to the austerity of your demand?
> I must set my face sternly towards truth
> as you turned toward Jerusalem, that all
> obedience should be shown us and accomplished.
> Your way to truth is hard, is dark, is pain.
> You have shown me the way, O Lord, but I
> am not prepared to bear your comfort.
> And yet, unwilling, unready, recalcitrant,
> I receive the flaming thrust that you have sent,
> and voices speaking as in my own tongue,
> and nothing will ever be the same again.[9]

Pentecost is very personal. Jesus says to each of us, "Receive the Holy Spirit." But he says those words to us as we are gathered in community, waiting together for God to do something in us and through us that we can't do by ourselves. Pentecost is communal.

We pray together for the grace to recognize in ourselves and in others the gifts bestowed on all of us by the Holy Spirit. And in the recognition we pray for the ability to forgive the times those gifts are squandered and for the times we fail to call them forth from each other.

Meetings, indeed any gathering of people, will always have a certain amount of tedium. But Pentecost is about synergy, about a shared experience that takes us all beyond our fears.

In his inaugural address, President John F. Kennedy told his country that the torch had been passed to a new generation. Today we celebrate Jesus' sharing of the Holy Spirit. Today the torch has been passed to us individually and collectively. Today I/we "receive the flaming thrust that you have sent/… and nothing will ever be the same again."

The Most Holy Trinity
John 3:16–18

✤ Once when Ignace Jan Paderewski, the famous Polish composer and pianist, was scheduled to play at a grand society event in the United States, a very unexpected incident took place. One of the stage hands had brought his young son to work with him and as he waited for his father in the wings, the boy grew bored.

He was drawn to the great shiny piano on the stage. He sat down at the piano and began playing "Chopsticks." There was quite an uproar from the surprised audience. When Paderewski heard the commotion he rushed on stage and, reaching around from behind the boy, he began to improvise a countermelody to "Chopsticks." As the two of them played together, Paderewski kept whispering in the boy's ear, "Keep going. Don't quit, son… don't stop…don't stop."

Today on this Feast of the Most Holy Trinity we hear Jesus tell his followers, "For God so loved the world that he gave his only Son, so that everyone who believes in him may not perish but may have eternal life."

Indeed, God did not send the Son into the world to condemn the world, but in order that the world might be saved through him." Jesus is trying to remind all of us that God engages with us and plays a counterpoint to the chopsticks that we play. Fumbling as our rendition of "Chopsticks" may be, God is reaching around from behind us and turning our lives into marvelous melodies.

In order to try to fathom this kind of relationship between God and all that God has created, we reflect today on the fact that God is relationship—a community of persons. In this relationship, called Trinity, we find a mutuality of persons, a kind of web of relationships characterized by intimacy.

Early Church councils and classical thinkers have tried to explain this relationship using Greek philosophical language. Later theologians have tried to shed new light on what we refer to as the doctrine of the Trinity. Today we ask how this mystery is connected to our relationship with God and the cosmos.

Part of our challenge comes from the fact that we keep trying with our finite language to name and understand an infinite mystery. Most of us probably grew up referring to God as Father, Son, and Holy Spirit.

Some prefer to say Creator, Redeemer, and Sanctifier. St. Augustine used the terms Lover, Beloved, and Loving. Perhaps today's Gospel passage is inviting us to put aside the naming and focus on relationship itself—God as a community of persons, God in relationship with us as human beings and, indeed, God in relationship with all that God has created. Madeleine L'Engle takes us right into the heart of relationship:

> Peace is the centre of the atom, the core
> Of quiet within the storm. It is not
> A cessation, a nothingness; more
> The lightning in reverse is what
> Reveals the light. It is the law that binds
> The atom's structure, ordering the dance
> Of proton and electron, and that finds

Within the midst of flame and wind, the glance
In the still eye of the vast hurricane.
Peace is not placidity: peace is
The power to endure the megatron of pain
With joy, the silent thunder of release,
The ordering of Love. Peace is the atom's start,
The primal image: God within the heart.[10]

We don't have to understand the mystery of the Most Holy Trinity because Jesus reminds us that "God so loved the world...." God who is Relationship resides within our hearts. So, no matter how we play the notes, today we listen as God whispers in our ears and in our hearts, "Keep going. Don't quit,...don't stop...don't stop."

Together with God we are co-creating the composition of our lives and co-redeeming all who hear the melody. All of this is possible because we believe in a God whose very essence is community.

Body and Blood of Christ
John 6:51–58

✢ "[F]or my flesh is true food and my blood is true drink. Those who eat my flesh and drink my blood abide in me, and I in them." As if this wasn't profound enough to occupy our minds and hearts for the rest of our lives, Jesus goes on to say, "[T]he one who eats this bread will live forever."

Our participation in the Eucharist, in the very life of Jesus, inaugurates our eternal life with God. It also relates us to each other. We share the Eucharist as a community of believers. The Eucharist is at once profoundly personal and deeply social.

What each of us brings to the celebration of the Eucharist is our own faith, nurtured by many, but dependent upon our personal efforts to grow in relationship with God.

There is a rarely told story related to the historic lunar walks that took place on July 20, 1969. Most are familiar with the words of Neil Armstrong as he walked on the surface of the moon for the first time: "That's one small step for man; one giant leap for mankind."

Few know that another small step took place shortly after the landing of Apollo 11. Buzz Aldrin, who remained aboard as pilot of the lunar module, said, "I'd like to take this opportunity to ask every person listening in, whoever and wherever they may be, to pause for a moment and contemplate the events of the past few hours and to give thanks in his or her own way." Then, in radio blackout, Aldrin took communion from a kit prepared by his pastor at Webster Presbyterian Church in Webster, Texas. Silently he gave thanks and ate.

What we bring to the Eucharist has far-reaching effects. We can never really celebrate the Eucharist alone. As Catholics, when we share the Body and Blood of Christ, we are sharing the same Body and Blood with Catholics gathered in places around the world. So, we are sharing the Eucharist with the people of India, Iraq, Ireland, Liberia, Peru, Iceland, and beyond.

None of us truly knows when and where we will share the Eucharist beyond today. Yet, there is a profound desire in each of us to bring our personal faith in Jesus' words, "Those who eat my flesh and drink my blood abide in me, and I in them," and lay it on the altar to be shared. Then, what a harvest there will be to gather and share as we each step into eternal life with God:

Once you dwelt in a country distant, unknown,
and foreign to me.
I passed my days in a land unheard of and unexplored by you.
You sowed wheat fields in your land,
while I tended vineyards in my home.
Fall after fall we reaped well,
but full barns and vats were not enough.
So we packed wheat and grapes enough to carry
and walked the roads from home.
You baked others bread; I poured them wine;
but I had no food, you no drink.

Each spring we'd stop on strange soil,
work it, sow it, and make it fruitful.
We'd stay until harvest time,
then make fresh bread and wine and move on.
We came by separate roads
one springtime to the same strange country.
When we harvested in fall I heard of your wheat,
you of my grapes.
You baked me fresh bread; I brought you new wine:
we ate and drank together.
When we leave this town by separate roads,
I'll take your wheat; you'll carry my grapes.
I'll sow your wheat near my vines,
and you'll plant my grapes next to your fields.
Then when others pour my wine, I can give them
your wheat's nourishment, too.
And when others break your bread,
you can offer the richness of my grapes.[11]

NOTES

1. Zimmerman, Irene, "Easter Witnesses," in *Incarnation*, (Cambridge: Cowley Publications, 2004), 112–113.
2. Theodulf of Orleans, "Wherefore the Scars of Christ's Passion Remained in the Body of His Resurrection," in *Divine Inspiration: The Life of Jesus in World Poetry*, edited by Robert Atwan, George Dardess, Peggy Rosenthal, (New York: Oxford University Press, 1998), 552–553.
3. Levertov, Denise, "The Servant-Girl at Emmaus (A Painting by Velázquez)," in *The Stream and the Sapphire*,(New York: New Directions Publishing Co., 1997), 43–44.
4. Lope de Vega Y Carpio, Felix, "Shepherd Who With Your Tender Calls," in *Divine Inspiration: The Life of Jesus in World Poetry*, edited by Robert Atwan, George Dardess, Peggy Rosenthal, (New York: Oxford University Press, 1998), 340.
5. Shea, John, "Prayer for a Nun in a Wheelchair," in *The Hour of the Unexpected*, Niles, IL: Argus Communications, 1977), 98.
6 Zimmerman, Irene, "I Am With You Always," in *Incarnation*, (Cambridge: Cowley Publications, 2004), 154–155.
7. Author Unknown, "Christ's Message," in *Inspiring Poems* compiled by C. B. Eavey (Grand Rapids: Zonderman Publishing House, 1970), 34.
8. Magee, Jr., John Gillespie, "High Flight," in *Poetry of the Spirit*, edited by Alan Jacobs (London, Watkins Publishing, 2002), 492.
9. L'Engle, Madeleine, "A man from Phrygia, on Pentecost," in *A Cry Like a Bell*, (Wheaton: Harold Shaw Publishers, 1987), 95.
10. L'Engle, Madeleine, "Sonnet, Trinity 18," in *The Weather of the Heart*, (Wheaton: Harold Shaw Publishers, 1978), 96.
11. Boehmer, Clare, ASC, "Two Pilgrims at Harvest Time," Unpublished. Used by permission of poet.